TOASTERS
1909·1960

TOASTERS
1909·1960

A LOOK AT THE INGENUITY AND DESIGN OF TOASTER MAKERS

E. Townsend Artman

77 Lower Valley Road, Atglen, PA 19310

ISBN: 0-88740-956-3
Printed in China

Published by Schiffer Publishing Ltd.
77 Lower Valley Road
Atglen, PA 19310
Please write for a free catalog.
This book may be purchased from
the publisher.
Please include $2.95 for shipping.
Try your bookstore first.

Library of Congress Cataloging-in-Publication Data

Artman, E. Townsend.
Toasters 1909-1960 / E. Townsend Artman.
p. cm. -- (A Schiffer book for collectors with values)
Includes bibliographical references and index.
ISBN 0-88740-956-3 (paper)
1. Electric toasters--Collectors and collecting--United
States--Catalogs. I. Title. II. Series: Schiffer book
for collectors with value guide.
TX657.T58A78 1996
683'.83'075--dc20 95-50312
CIP

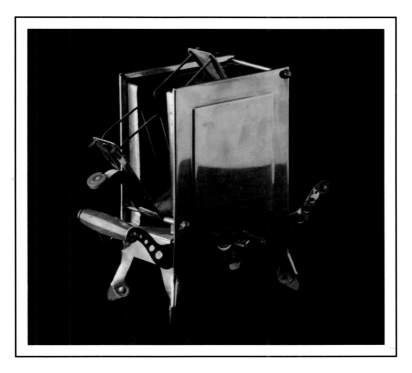

HISTORICAL DATE DISCLAIMER

◆

The dates shown in this book are as accurate as we know them. Some sources unintentionally quote dates that are tainted with hype and also confuse patent dates with manufacture dates. In the "Toaster Wars" of the early years misinformation was the rule, and much of that misinformation has found its way into publications. We will try not to do this. However, accurate records are difficult to come by and patent dates stamped on toasters often don't refer to the toaster, but some special part of it that may have been invented years earlier than the toaster. They also may remain on the toaster long after their 17 year life span. Clear photographs of the toaster have been provided, as well as its label, and if no more accurate date is known, the label information will be used. In some cases we will use no date at all. Accurate historical information that pertains to the America Toaster would be very much welcomed.

—The Author

To my wife Catherine who has gone to countless flea markets with me, even when she didn't want to. I love her.

Acknowledgments

Joe Lukach, a fellow toaster enthusiast, helped me tremendously in preparing this book. He gave his extensive knowledge of toaster dates, names of toasters, and most of all allowed me to photograph toasters from his collection that I didn't have in my own. He also graciously accepted my crazed phone calls when I needed some information. Thanks Joe, your patience and kind help is very much appreciated.

Bill Blakeslee, another toaster collector whom I found via the internet, supplied articles, found reference books when I couldn't, and also gave of his knowledge willingly. Thanks Bill.

TABLE
OF
CONTENTS

INTRODUCTION

When you tell people you collect old toasters, they do a slow-motion pause, look at you very seriously and kinda not knowing what to say utter these words, "Ahh, do you like toast?" It never fails—everyone always asks the same question. Sometimes there's a nervous little laugh on the end but it's always the same question.

In most people's minds there's something basically wrong with collecting toasters. That chrome box that sat on the breakfast table every morning just seems too mundane, too everyday, too too...*uncollectible*. Well hold on to your hats boys and girls you're going to see toasters you never dreamed existed. Toasters that look like 16th century German armor, ones that have delicate flowers on their porcelain bases, and some of the dumbest Rube Goldberg machines that any designer ever created.

I got hooked on toasters in the late 80s, I thought I'd just buy one, once. Well you can't just buy one, once. You can't get off that easy. You have to get that second one and when you get that second one, you, my friend, have a collection. Now "Toaster Madness" sets in. Forget any sanity you might have once had and learn to answer that question with a toothy smile and a sincere, "Why yes, I like toast very much, thank you."

This book celebrates the wacky collector in each of us and explores the invention of the American Toaster starting at a time when there was no federal deficit, bread was a nickel a loaf, and the American Industrial Designer was on the cusp of tremendous successes. In this newly electrified era the idea of a separate appliance used for one purpose and only that purpose was a new and strange one, and was to change the eating habits of America. Toaster companies boasted of preparing a hot breakfast without heating up the stove. Cooking breakfast at the table was impossible until now unless you planted your plate on the stove itself and ate hovering over a hot burner. Well, now things changed in a hurry. Toaster companies designed toasters that timed the toast, rang bells, shut the heat down, made coffee, cooked waffles, poached eggs, fried bacon, and really became small stoves on your breakfast table. American women would start to unshackle themselves from the kitchen stove, but only ever so slightly. Later decades would have to complete the process.

Toasters haven't been a very popular item to collect until recently. They were thought of as only utilitarian appliances—not something that may show some style or intrigue or value. Maybe they just needed a catalog to show them off. Maybe they, like many collectibles, have been biding their time waiting in some dusty attic until discovered by the unsuspecting. Well, they're collectible now, they're hot, no pun intended, and their prices are rising.

So, the next time you are at a flea market or antique store and you see a toaster (yes, it will be on the floor or on the ground under the display table) give it a second glance. Go ahead and pick it up, pretend that it doesn't interest you much, and laugh with your friend at how silly it is for people to collect dumb things like toasters. Let your friend walk away. Then caress the slick chrome, play with the timer, fiddle with the thermostat, work the mechanism, work the flopping, dropping, popping, turning, sliding, tipping, zipping. A smile will come to your face and your hand will go to your wallet. Welcome to Toaster Land.

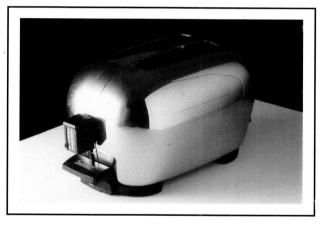

Fat Man

MY FIRST TOASTER

I bought my first old toaster in 1987, it was a Toastermaster 1A3 and it cost me nine bucks. I wasn't going to collect toasters, I just liked the way it looked, all industrial revolution-like, heavy, uncompromising, no frills, except for its timer. It sorta said "I can toast the pants off all those plastic impostors." It had but one slot to put the bread into, not two like *normal*. I surmised that was so it could concentrate on doing a great job, one thing at a time. It didn't heat up TV dinners or open its mouth wide to engulf bagels and English muffins. It was made to do one thing well, turn bread into toast. And... it didn't work.

Well, it sorta worked but it was quirky. It heated up, but shut down right away, then sometimes the timer stopped and it didn't pop up and I was rewarded with the screeching of the smoke alarm and you couldn't see your hand in front of your face. It still looked like it could do a great job though, maybe I could fix it. Here's where the collection starts.

My No. 1

I'm fairly mechanically minded, after all, I did flunk out of one of the best engineering schools in the country. So, I broke out my toolbox and started in unscrewing things, bending metal tabs back, basically having a look inside. This was gonna be a "Sunday afternoon project," one that gets done in three hours with near instant gratification. The outer chrome case came off without a hitch and there lay the heart of the toaster, the heating element, beside that was the timer and the pushdown lever. All in between the metal maze covering every crack and crevice were the remains of, of...other people's toast. Yuck. Parts were glued together with burned crumbs and a kind of stiff grease that clogged

the timer and stuck to the inner works. Where'd the grease come from? Oh no, other people's butter! It started to come back to me, my son laying his buttered toast on top of our toaster to melt the cold butter. Did other people do that too? Here was proof that they did. I instinctively knew what to do, I had to eradicate every single greasy crumb, making my toaster, *my* toaster.

The timer, a brass mechanism that has all the delicate parts of a clock except for the hands, was the worst offender. The gears had cut neat grooves in the semi-hardened grease and there was a little drop of oil forming on the big loop on the mainspring. Maybe I should forget it and not take the clock apart.

As the main spring went "sprong" and propelled a gear out of its metal cage bouncing it off the wall, I wished I had decided that erratic toast making was an elegant game between you and your toaster. Not something to be messed with.

Two hundred toasters later, I can take 'em apart, fix 'em and put 'em back together like a "Sunday afternoon project." But fixing a toaster isn't much fun unless the toaster is. What makes it fun is the look and design of the little heater. Some were constructed of cheap, thin metal, with no concern for quality. Surprisingly though many of these embody the wackiest, most avant-garde designs. Most companies produced excellent quality toasters that could last a life time. You probably remember the one and only toaster your parents made toast with every morning. I'll bet it still works today, unless you filled it full of crumbs and butter.

TOASTER HISTORY

The electric toaster was born in 1909 and was named D-12. This model was made into three variations. Toaster collectors must have one of these to even be considered collectors.

At the turn of the century electricity was still a very new thing and many ideas were being tried to produce heat or light from an electric wire. Thomas Alva Edison's early experiments with the electric light bulb were attempts to solve the same problems faced by toaster inventors—namely how to invent a wire that would heat up and cool down many times without oxidizing and burning up. A thin electrified iron wire produces a lot of heat and light and is excellent for singeing bread or reading by. Regrettably the wire burns out quickly. Much time had been spent trying to solve this problem. Edison had tried thousands of kinds of filaments and had sent his agents far and wide, from the jungles of the Amazon to the forests of Japan searching for exotic materials. Finally, he came upon the idea of using a simple cotton sewing thread. It was burned, placed in a vacuum, and with the current running through it, it glowed for a long time. It glowed all night. The vacuum acted as an insulator from the air and avoided meltdown. Electric irons were in some use by this time and had wires imbedded in a plaster material, a similar concept to Edison's light bulb, the wire avoiding the air. Even armed with this knowledge it was years before the first successful toaster came into being. The inventors knew that they, like Edison, needed to somehow shield the wire from the air to avoid oxidation.

But it took the young inventor Albert L. Marsh from Lake Bluff, Illinois, to find a new solution. On February 6, 1906, he was granted a patent for his discovery of a miracle alloy that would not oxidize and burn up after many thousands of heating and cooling cycles. The alloy was a combination of chromium and nickel. It heated up hot but didn't burn out. Basically it worked.

The first hurdle was solved—they had a reliable source of heat.

George Schneider of American Electric Heater Co. Detroit, Michigan, was granted a toaster patent July 17, 1906, five months after the Marsh wire patent. Some sources suggest that Marsh and Schneider knew each other because the toaster patent called for a non-oxidizing wire in its mechanical description. I have never seen this toaster and can not be sure that it got past the drawing stages. It is generally agreed that the General Electric 1909 D-12 is the granddaddy (or grandmother) of the modern toaster. It carried a patent date of 10-20-08 but this referred to the resistance wire, its element, rather than the toaster patent. This wire contained iron in an effort to avoid the Marsh patent. The first version of this toaster was marketed in 1909 and applied for patent in July 1909. Another patent date February 22, 1910, is the date carried by version number two. Number three, the last, came a year later.

The American Toaster was a great invention that opened up new opportunities in this narrow avenue of industrial design. The designers would be taking a new idea, an appliance that could cook a hot breakfast at the table, and have a field day with its physical appearance and its function. They sculpted it, gave it the look of the automobile of the day, streamlined it like the Norfolk & Western Cannonball Express, hid marvelous mechanisms inside to manipulate the toast, built clocks to turn it on and off, heat sensors to regulate the browning, conveyer systems to provide a smooth ride, spring loaded ones that gave cartoonists ammunition for their strips, and generally went design wacky with this hot wire breakfast maker.

Burned Toast

THE EVOLUTION OF
THE AMERICAN TOASTER

◆

Early Days: A green stick held over a fire was probably the first toaster. Later came the iron fork. Wire and tinware racks standing on the wood or gas stove was the toaster just before electricity was available. These devises were just stands that kept the bread from falling over, they provided no heat.

1882: First distribution of electricity. Thomas Alva Edison's first station on Pearl Street in New York City.

1905-1906: Albert Marsh invents the chromium-nickel resistance wire, Ni-Chrome. It's still the heating element of toasters even today. George Schneider invents and patents a toaster. The patent is under the name of the American Electric Heater Co., Detroit. Not successful if ever marketed.

1908: General Electric patents its own resistance wire. The "Toaster Wars" start, everybody claims they were first with some new patentable breakthrough.

1909: GE introduces the first commercially successful toaster the D-12. It was the first of three versions, basically just a wire stand with a heating element, but an *electric* heating element. It carried a 10-20-'08 patent date which referred to GE's resistance wire, not the toaster. Westinghouse invents a horizontal toaster with a heating element made like a flat iron.

1912: A wire device that turned the toast over automatically was patented by Spencer Wiltsie. The toaster failed for other reasons, however. The Copeman Electric Stove Co. was assigned the patent.

1913: Copeman puts the auto turning design (just some bent wires, but an elegant solution) into existing toasters. It was Mrs. Copeman's idea, incidentally. The first to display this feature was the Turn-over Toaster by Westinghouse. This was a major advance and many other manufacturers jumped on the bandwagon attempting to invent their own design while trying to avoid patent infringements. It was a squabble and added more confusion to the early Toaster Wars.

1915: GE granted a design patent for the X-2 an experimental model using an iron wire encased in an insulating material. It was much like the element in electric stoves of today. Some misinformation exists as to the accuracy of the manufacturing date. GE's advertising department dated this model 1905, but this is probably just another attempt to avoid someone else's patents.

1917-1920: First "Turner/Swinger" patented, a rotating basket was turned manually to toast the second side. Frank Collier patent.

1918: Armstrong Electric introduces the first combo toaster, the Perc-O-Toaster, billed as "Coffee and toast made at the table." There was an optional waffle maker attachment available which truly made this appliance versatile. A breakfast of coffee, toast or waffles, without firing up the kitchen stove, and all made at the table, was a liberating and new idea. Charles Strite patents the first automatic Pop-Up for restaurant use.

1920s: The ubiquitous "Flopper" comes on to the scene with many companies offering a similar mechanical solution for holding and turning the bread. Unfortunately the first maker is unrecorded. These toasters all worked pretty much the same. The doors leaned together at the top forming an "A" and are hinged at the bottom, when opened they kind of flop down and the toast fell over on to the open door. Some models would even turn the toast over automatically when you closed the door. This design persisted for many years. It was simple and performed well.

◆

1922: Estate Stove Company flips out the first family four slicer. It was a square model with four doors. When you opened one door the rest would flip around simultaneous and turn the toast. First oven style toaster offered by Best Stove and Stamping Company, Detroit. It held two slices vertically in an open drawer that you shoved into a metal box where the element toasted the bread. When you thought the toast was done, you yanked the drawer out.

1924: The first home automatic toaster announced: (*Automatic*: To limit the browning of the bread by selecting a predetermined cooking time). It sported a dial, much like a telephone and the dial regulated the toasting time. D.A. Rogers of South Minneapolis, Minnesota, was the inventor but his toaster was a flop and faded from the scene. The horizontal toaster/table stove by the Chicago Flexible Shaft Company (later to become Sunbeam) was introduced. You could cook an egg on it too. Another combo unveiled, but this time one item it cooked was a non-breakfast food. It was a popcorn/toaster duo made by Acme Electric and Manufacturing Company, Cleveland, Ohio.

1926: Waters Genter Company (soon to become McGraw Electric Company then McGraw-Edison Company) markets the first commercially successful automatic toaster and dubs it "Toastmaster." It was the first home "Pop-Up" and had a timer that shut the heat off and ejected the toast when done. Single slice only. Nickel plated. Later the finish was chrome.

1929: George Curtiss granted a design patent on the stunning pearl drop earring Swinger, the Universal E9410. Truly a spectacular design.

1930: First non ticking timer used by Proctor Electric Company (later Proctor-Silex Corporation). A bimetal strip (two strips of different metals bonded together) was used to gauge the desired toasting time. The strip, inside the hot toaster, absorbed the heat unevenly and expanded more on one side than the other. This bent the strip and triggered the current shutdown. It made no noise until it rang the bell, signaling the toast was done. It worked like a stealth toaster.
The "Dropper" was first introduced by Beardsley and Wolcott Manufacturing Company, of Waterbury, Connecticut. Works much like a pop-up toaster in China. It drops the toast. A trap door drops the toast and it falls down onto a built-in tray under the toaster.

1937: First conveyer system used to move bread slices continuously through the toaster heating box. It was named the "Toast-O-Lator" of Toast-O-Lator Company in New York. Bread went in one end and toast came out the other. Good-bye bread, hello toast. Very complicated mechanics. Most still work today.

1940: First toaster to feature a "keep warm" selection. The heat was shut off by the timer, and the toast was held inside staying warm until you manually popped it up. Made by GE.

1947: First "Long Slot" toaster introduced. A pop-up with one long opening that accommodated two slices of bread standing edge to edge. Samson United Corporation.

1949: Sensors: Sunbeam first to use a devise that could measure the amount of heat reflected off the toast and sensed when it was done. It then popped up and shut off.

1955: GE introduces a two slice, long slot toaster with a drawer in the bottom used to heat or toast other foods.

1959: GE equips their toaster with a double pole main switch, an innovative safety idea that guarded against shock.

1960: Nothing much happened, the Grand Age of the Toaster was over and it was stretching at the end. Enter a lot of cheaply made and badly designed plastic numbers that show up at garage sales six months after they are bought. These will be collected also.

TOASTER PATTERNS

*Each Toaster Brands its
Distinctive Mark on the Bread*

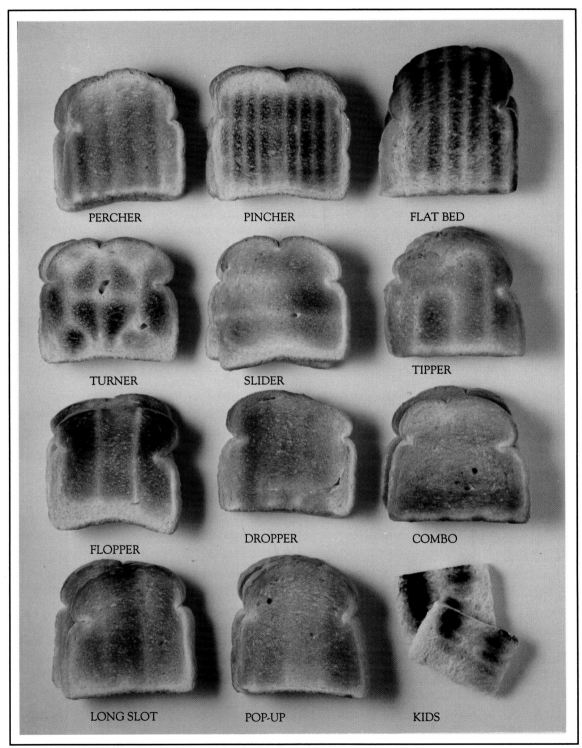

PERCHER

PINCHER

FLAT BED

TURNER

SLIDER

TIPPER

FLOPPER

DROPPER

COMBO

LONG SLOT

POP-UP

KIDS

A TRIP TO THE
FLEA MARKET

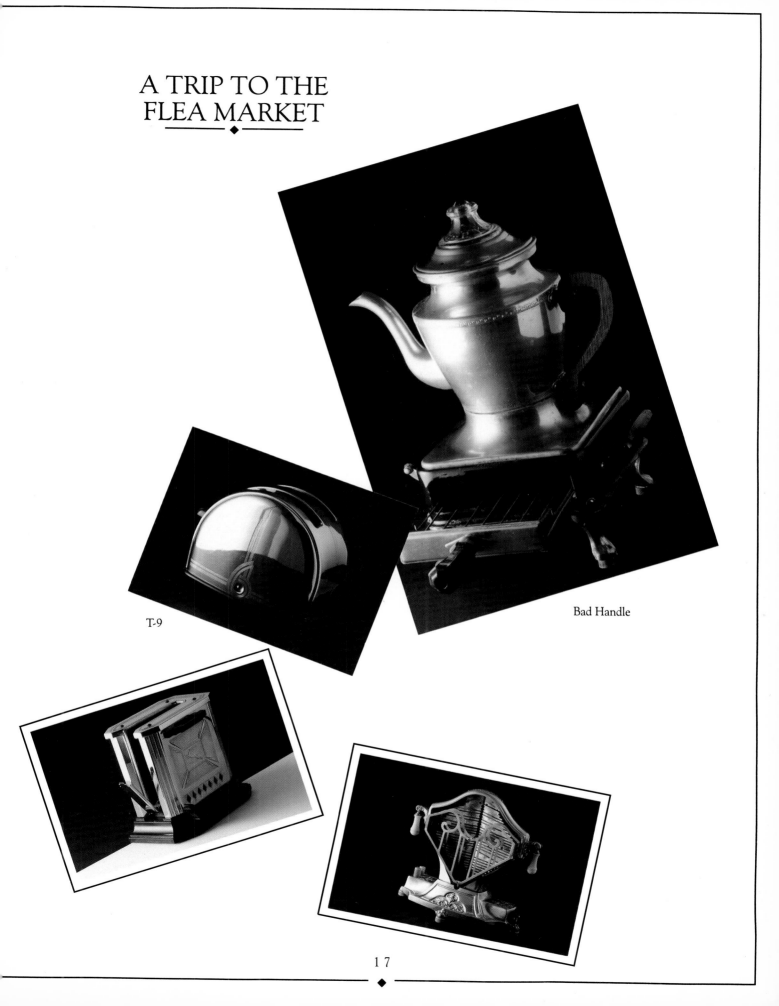

T-9

Bad Handle

I collect old electric toasters. To find them, I sometimes get up at six o'clock Sunday morning to go to a flea market. The drive is usually one or two hours from wherever I am, regardless of where I am. It seems as if I'm in the center of a big circle with flea markets on the outskirts always a few hours away, never in the town I'm in. This of course adds more tension and delay to the toaster search. Many times my wife Catherine goes with me but then we leave later. She often suggests we stop and grab a quick breakfast, just a yogurt or even a packaged sweet roll from a gas station. "It won't take two minutes," she pleads. I ignore her and drive on. She becomes listless, noticeably pale and has trouble talking. I finally get it. Bounding out of the Amoco station I jam the blueberry yogurt through her open window and peel out. I'm in a big sweat fearing that someone has snatched up that special toaster before I got there, a Mesco or maybe a Porcelier. This is not some relaxing day browsing the antique tents, chit-chatting with the geeks, this is serious business and we're late. Late.

After 96 minutes of Indy 500 driving we arrive at the fairgrounds hot and sweaty in our non air-conditioned Civic. The tension increases as we get closer to the parking area. Catherine asks me for a quarter, I don't respond.

We drive down the road leading to the admission stand. The line of cars crawls, each having to stop at the stand and pay their money. A bored kid sits on a creosoted post taking the entrance fee, he struggles to make correct change even though the price is in whole dollars. Each car has to stop and take part in the math lesson. I'm claustrophobic, I need outta here. The van in front of us finally rolls past the kid, now it's my turn. I shove the six bucks out the car window towards the bored kid. He takes it, not making eye contact, and utters a robotic "Have a nice day." We're in.

Inching onto the grass and mud parking lot I encounter teenage parking boys wearing red hats and shirts. They are directing cars to park in precise spots in predetermined rows. They laugh and joke with one another but direct none of this humor towards us. They display a certain controlling attitude and seem to enjoy stopping the snail like line to inflict their will on the poor patrons, "You park over here, no not there, here, right here," they say, with a sly smile and a wink to their partners. Then moving to the next victim slowing the line of cars ever so slightly they

hold up one hand in a "stop" gesture and gaze intently across the far cornfield absorbed in some important imaginary parking problem. Seizing this inattentive moment, I take off. I boot it! I roar past 'em all. They assume the "wait-a-minute-I'm-in-control-here" posture, by bringing their hands smartly to their hips like they're gonna do something. As we race by, "Haaay!!" finally squeezes out of their mouths. Glaring at us just long enough to still appear powerful they shrug and resume their fun. They don't run after us, don't use their walkey-talkeys, they just forget it. They're back to slowing the line and alternate between jokes on each other and stern looks at the cars. As we bounce across the field I duck my head to avoid slamming it into the roof. We're on our own. We're free. Catherine grabs for a napkin to wipe the yogurt off her pants and blouse.

We race towards the front of the lot, but find no space we can fit in. Up and down the lines of cars there's no break between them. My face starts to itch. I just know some collector's fondling that special toaster or worse some lady's buying it 'cause it's *different.* or *cute.* Careening down the number two aisle I see an opening. It's the last spot in the row and next to it is a little incline. It looks a little muddy, well, it looks really muddy, but it's the only parking place in a half mile. Noticing a car turning into our lane, I gun it! We politely cut him off but hit the mud a little too fast and the car slides slightly broadside, cutting deep furrows in the mud, I wrestle with the wheel, we squeeze past the Chevy and come to a stop leaning a little up hill. It's fine, no problem. I step out and slog through the mud. Catherine, imitating a high wire walker, steps over the muddy ruts and loses her balance.

The temperature's in the 90s and the humidity is unbearable. We shuffle along with the swarm of people past the building labeled Sheep, and there before us lay hundreds of tents, tables of stuff, junk everywhere, maybe we weren't too late, maybe it was still here. I was hot and delighted.

Cruising the rows with an eye peeled for shiny things I got a flash from a booth filled with depression glass. I didn't get a good look but it seemed like it was a toaster. Squeezing through the crowd I got closer and realized it was really a heater that plumbers use to heat up a soldering iron. That was OK I've often mistaken a truck mirror for a late model Toastmaster. The day was still young and we'd just arrived. Catherine buys a green depression ware cream pitcher as I look down the line for the next possibility.

Hours go by. We stumble past each booth filled with people, strollers, crying babies, and hundreds of items piled on top of each other, and sadly all barren of toasters. I've been to the flea market many a time and settled for an old BB gun, or something, but the potential to come home with a Commander, a D12, or even a good duplicate sort of fades as the hot afternoon wears on. I didn't want another BB gun. My legs aching and my neck sunburned, we searched on.

I'm depressed and in a snippy mood. My wife tries to get me out of it by being very chipper and talking about anything she can think of that I might find interesting. "Let's go." I say. She disguises her elation and agrees since she had had enough of this two hours ago and besides I'm impossible by now.

Trudging back past aisles we've already seen I think I see something. It looked promising, although most anything would now, but I can't quite see it clearly. It is! It's a toaster all right, AND one I'd never seen. Nickel plated, red bakelite handles, It looks like a dropper with a hot plate. It's beautiful. It's unknown to me. Like a welcome newcomer. I reach down to bring it closer to see what hidden bells, what special timers, what innovating idea it displayed to make bread into toast. I reach out almost touching the back handle when a pudgy hand darts between my hand and the toaster. This is where it starts to all be in slow motion.

Turning my head in a fuzzy slurring motion a red hat comes into view, a red shirt slides by, and I see a guy. He holds the toaster in his hands, in his hands. I don't have it, he has it. Lifting my eyes from the toaster I recognized him for the first time. He's the kid, the attendance kid, the one on the post. He had my toaster in his hands. What could he possibly want from it? It's not for kids. Given my experience at these kinds of markets, I pretended not to have tried to pick up the toaster at all and picked up the chrome Mac ashtray instead, showing no interest in the toaster at all. He has a buddy with him who sports the same red hat and shirt, another parking boy. The new boy is encouragingly not interested in some old toaster, he wants lunch and urges the kid to go with him. This doesn't persuade him to put the toaster down. He is somehow transfixed. I've seen it before, he has to have it. He's become a

Toaster Boy. He holds the toaster up to the dealer as if to inquire its price. Instinct takes over, I push him aside and immediately start to negotiate the price on the ashtray. I make a big scene with the dealer about how I'm very interested in collecting Mac ashtrays but don't know much about them and would like to learn more. The dealer says he doesn't know anything about them either. I pay the twenty eight dollars for the ashtray. Then it happens, toaster boy is still holding up my toaster and he says to his uninterested friend, "Doesn't this look cool?" The other responds, "Well it's different, let's eat!" "I'll meet'cha in a minute," he says and asks the dealer the price. "Twelve dollars." I'm petrified and mute. My experience vanishes and I blurt out to the kid, "Whadda ya gonna do with that old toaster, ya know it don't work." The kid looks at me and snarls, "Who are you mister?" Now what? I didn't expect this. The dealer stares at me with dagger eyes, I'm ruining his sale. I fall back, staggering watching the kid pull a twenty from his pocket and give it to the dealer. My toaster is wrapped in newspaper and shoved into a used brown sack. It ain't going home with me. The kid walks a few feet away, stops, slowly turns, and with a pensive look on his face starts back for the dealer's table. Has he had second thoughts? Can I still own it? Returns aren't a part of Flea Market tradition, but I'd slide in with a quiet profitable offer, the dealer would be happy, the kid would get his money back, and I'd get my toaster. A good thing all around. I strided forward with the swagger of knowing the out come in a poker hand. Why if the dealer didn't want it back I could reason with the new Toaster Boy and tell him I'm a collector and I need it for my collection and I'd pay him a big profit and he'd say OK and sell it to me. Any smart kid would understand the value to a collector and making a big profit too, I'd reason with him.

The kid pushes through the newly formed crowd, calls the dealer and holds up his change, a five and three ones. The dealer looks up from his latest deal. The kid said, "Haay, I thought you said this was twelve bucks, you only gave me eight back." I knew I was beat, I went home.

PERCHERS

Bread Stands Alone

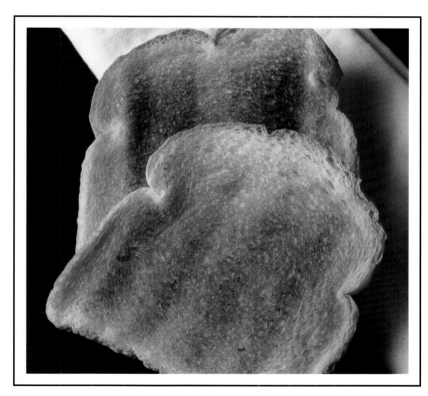

1

1909-10 GENERAL ELECTRIC
MODEL D-12
TWO SLICES

The granddaddy of all toasters, the D-12 was the first available home toaster. Its patent was applied for July, 1909. The photo shows the second in the series of three. The first one had twelve vertical wires to support the toast and the sides of the basket were closed with wire. It was hard to get the toast out. Sadly I don't own the first one. All versions were very well made with porcelain bases, an excellent insulator and selling point in the new and scary days of home electricity. The date carried on the base October 20, 1908 refers to the patent on the wire element not the toaster.

Produces crisp toast marked with a vertical pattern. No volts, watts, or amps designated on toaster.

Thanks to Doug Huse

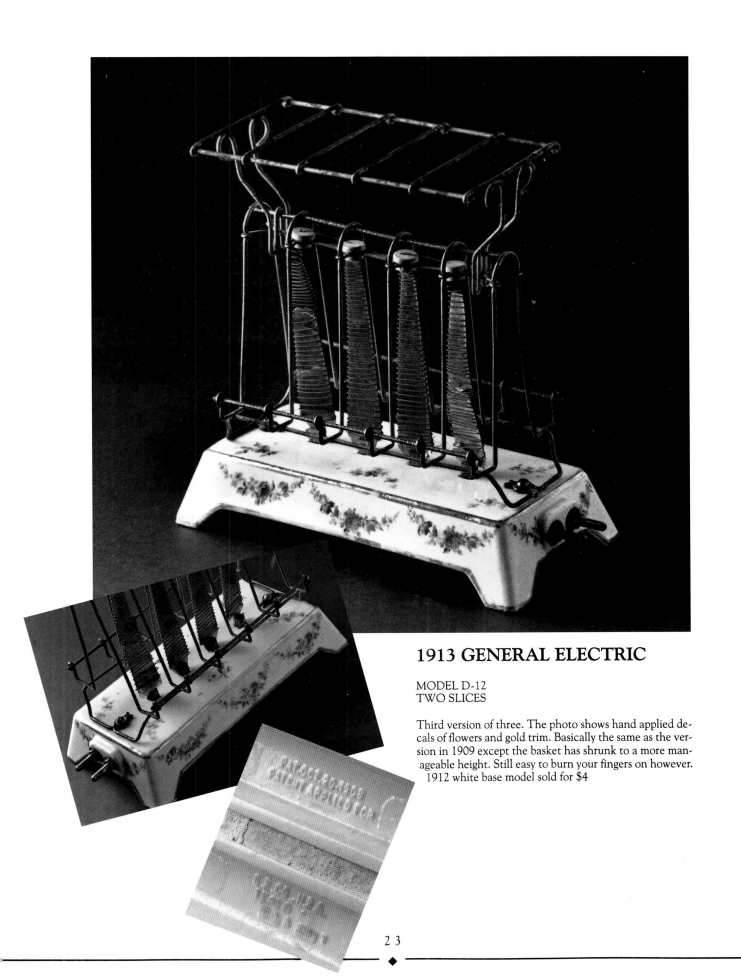

1913 GENERAL ELECTRIC

MODEL D-12
TWO SLICES

Third version of three. The photo shows hand applied decals of flowers and gold trim. Basically the same as the version in 1909 except the basket has shrunk to a more manageable height. Still easy to burn your fingers on however.
1912 white base model sold for $4

1909 SIMPLEX

SIMPLEX ELECTRIC HEATING COMPANY, BOSTON,
MASSACHUSETTS
MODEL T-211: 104-112 VOLTS 4 AMPS TWO SLICES

Very heavy (4 lbs.), well made toaster. Featured doors that
regulated the heat as well as how crisp or moist the toast
was. Cast iron base. Early models had ceramic core element. Patent application October, 1909.
1912 sold for $5 and in 1920 for $9.50

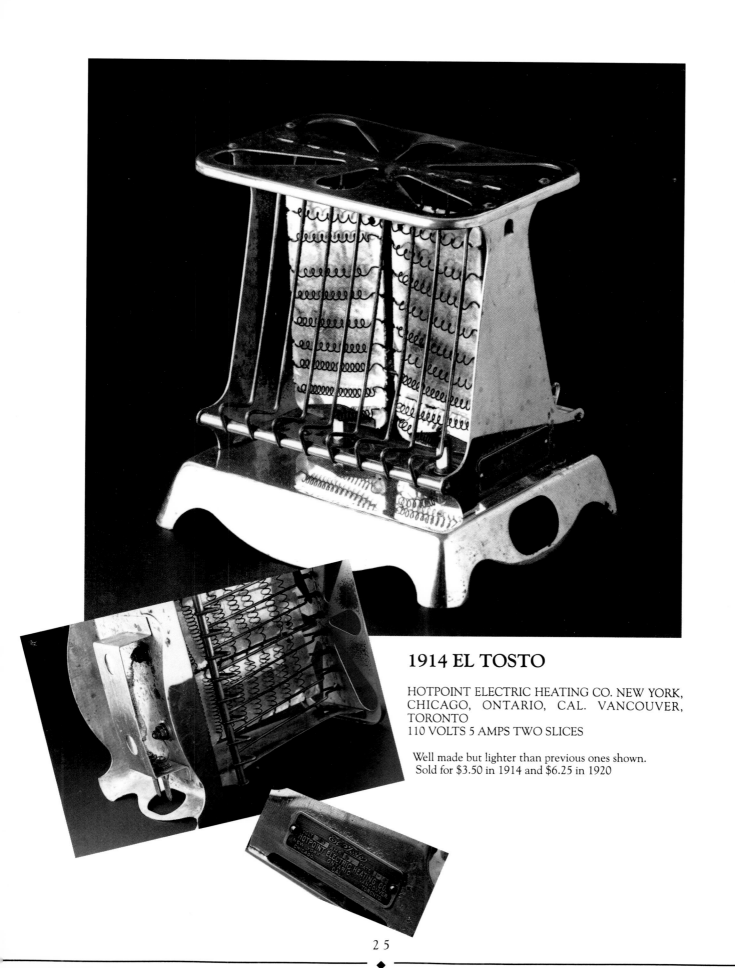

1914 EL TOSTO

HOTPOINT ELECTRIC HEATING CO. NEW YORK,
CHICAGO, ONTARIO, CAL. VANCOUVER,
TORONTO
110 VOLTS 5 AMPS TWO SLICES

Well made but lighter than previous ones shown.
Sold for $3.50 in 1914 and $6.25 in 1920

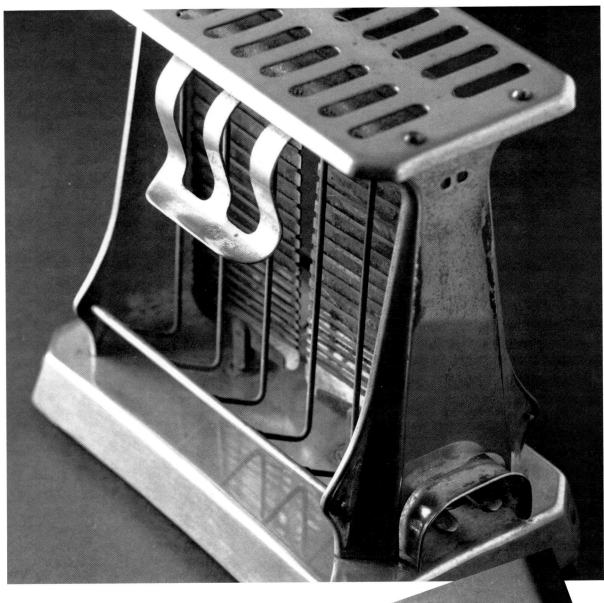

1915 HOTPOINT

EDISON ELECTRIC APPLIANCE CO. NEW YORK,
CHICAGO, ONTARIO, CAL
NO. 114T5 110 VOLTS 450 WATTS TWO SLICES

Has a toast holder hinged on the top. The bread was pushed
up into the holder where it was held by the weight of the
holder not by any spring devise. The holder got hot so it
was wise not to touch it. Toasted crisp toast fast.

1918 PELOUZE VERTICAL TOASTER

PELOUZE MANUFACTURING CO., CHICAGO
PATENTED OCT. 31, 1911 SEPT. 10, 1912 110 VOLTS 500 WATTS TWO SLICES

Sturdy, heavy design with stylish feet.
Courtesy of Joe Lukach

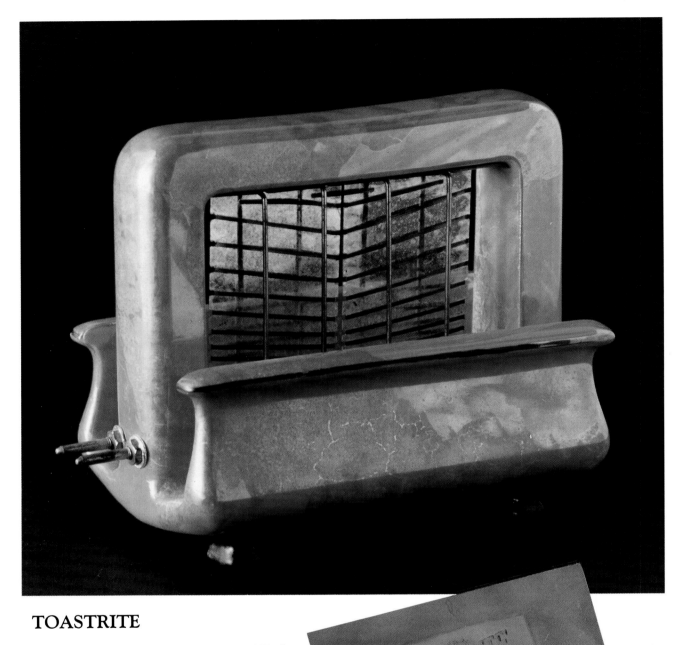

TOASTRITE

THE PAN ELECTRIC MFG. CO., CLEVELAND, O.
PATENTED 110 VOLTS 500 WATTS TWO SLICES

These beautiful toasters came in five colors, including the
Blue Willow Pattern shown next. They are extremely hard
to find, owing to a limited number being made, and after
all they are made of breakable porcelain.

Courtesy of Joe Lukach

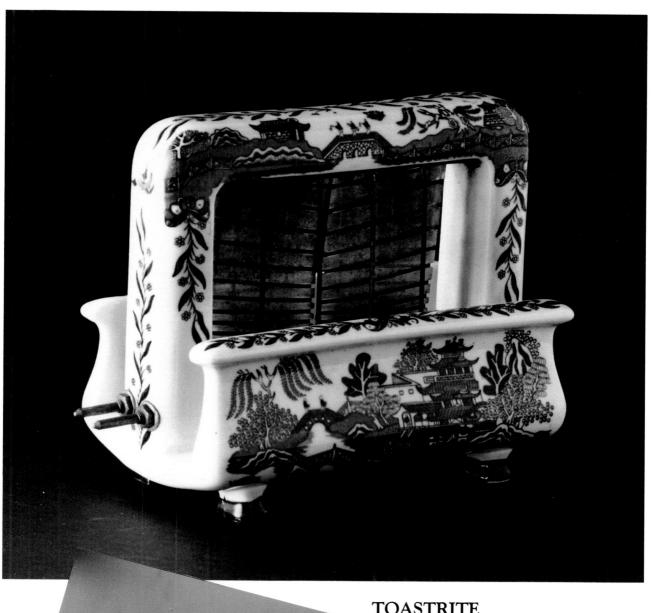

TOASTRITE

THE PAN ELECTRIC MFG. CO., CLEVELAND, O.
PATENTED 110 VOLTS 500 WATTS TWO SLICES

The Blue Willow Pattern was not only used on this toaster,
but on a whole matching breakfast set. Be still my heart.

PINCHERS

Bread Pinched on a Perch

2

1912 UNIVERSAL

LANDERS, FRARY & CLARK NEW BRIT-
AIN, CONN. U.S.A.
NO. E941 110 VOLTS 3.1 AMPS TWO
SLICES

Very light toaster, less than a pound, but well
made. Spring clamps hold bread tightly against
the patented three part element.
Sold for $4 in 1914 and $5 for silver

SIMPLEX

NO. T 212 104-112 VOLTS 4 AMPS

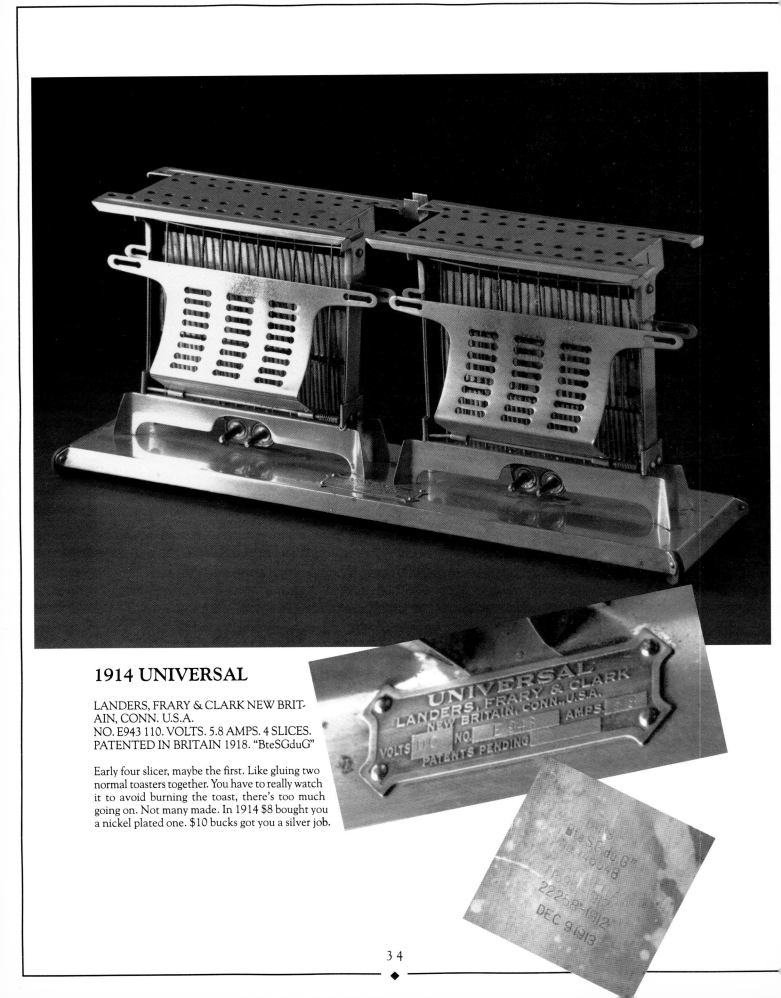

1914 UNIVERSAL

LANDERS, FRARY & CLARK NEW BRIT-
AIN, CONN. U.S.A.
NO. E943 110. VOLTS. 5.8 AMPS. 4 SLICES.
PATENTED IN BRITAIN 1918. "BteSGduG"

Early four slicer, maybe the first. Like gluing two
normal toasters together. You have to really watch
it to avoid burning the toast, there's too much
going on. Not many made. In 1914 $8 bought you
a nickel plated one. $10 bucks got you a silver job.

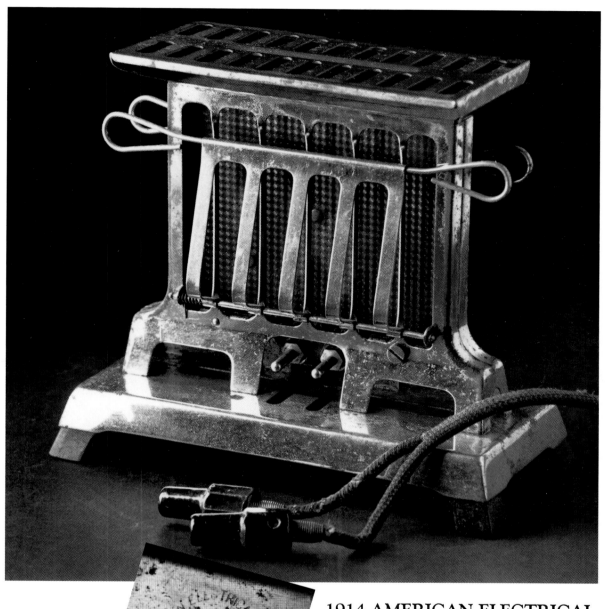

1914 AMERICAN ELECTRICAL HEATER CO.

NO. 5825. CARRIES LMP DIAMOND. PATENTED 1912-1916. TWO SLICES

This early model uses a heating element much like an electric iron. In fact this company made the American Beauty Iron. A stamped metal laminate of mica and sheet steel with the flat resistance wire running through it comprised this unique heating element. Note the connecting terminal sockets, separate for each pole, and made of porcelain. The art silk cord is a deep crimson color. Another well made toaster. The photo depicts an example sold in 1916 surprisingly still using the sandwich element.

AMERICAN BEAUTY TOASTER

AMERICAN ELECTRICAL HEATER CO.
NO. 5825G. CARRIES LMP DIAMOND.
PATENTED 1912-1915. TWO SLICES

This version, identical to the 5825 above
except for its element and brand name,
carries a date one year earlier. I don't
know why, but I'm relatively sure the
5825G came second because of the more
modern element and the "G" designation.
Did they exist at the same time?

HANDY HOT

CHICAGO ELECTRIC MFG. CO. 110 VOLTS. 500 WATTS. TWO SLICES

Inexpensively made. Light in weight. This example is starting to lose its plating. It toasts quite well but gets very hot.

1918-1923 UNIVERSAL

LANDERS, FRARY & CLARK. NEW BRIT-
AIN, CONN. U.S.A.
NO. E945. 106-114 VOLTS. 3.1 AMPS.
PATENT DATES 1912-1918. LMP DIAMOND
WITH RESISTANCE WIRE PATENT DATE
FEB. 6, 1906

One of the classics. A very well made toaster, with
three part element, and cast base. This model shows
the elegant toast warming rack which is reminiscent
of a king's or queen's crown. Early models were nickel
on brass, later chrome on steel.
$6.85 in 1919. $7.50 in 1924.

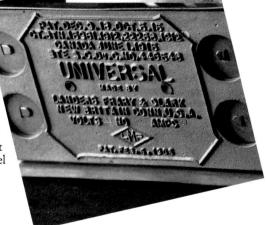

1918-1928 UNIVERSAL

LANDERS, FRARY & CLARK. NEW BRITAIN, CONN. U.S.A.
NO. E946. 106-114 VOLTS. 3.1 AMPS. PATENT DATES 1912-1915. LMP DIAMOND WITH RESISTANCE WIRE PATENT DATE FEB. 6, 1906

Has heavy cast base and three part element. Porcelain knobs may have been added by the owner as I haven't seen them on other models and they are a great addition for cooler fingers.
Priced at $6.25 in 1919.

NATIONAL STAMPING & ELECTRIC WORKS

MADE IN U.S.A. CHICAGO.
NO. 230. 110 VOLTS. 5 AMPS. TWO SLICES

Fairly well made.

1925-1929 UNIVERSAL

LANDERS, FRARY & CLARK. NEW BRIT-
AIN, CONN.
NO. E948T. 106-114 VOLTS. 5.5
AMPS. TWO SLICES

Nice pierced design, of excellent construction. Nickeled brass.

FLAT BEDS

Toast Siesta

3

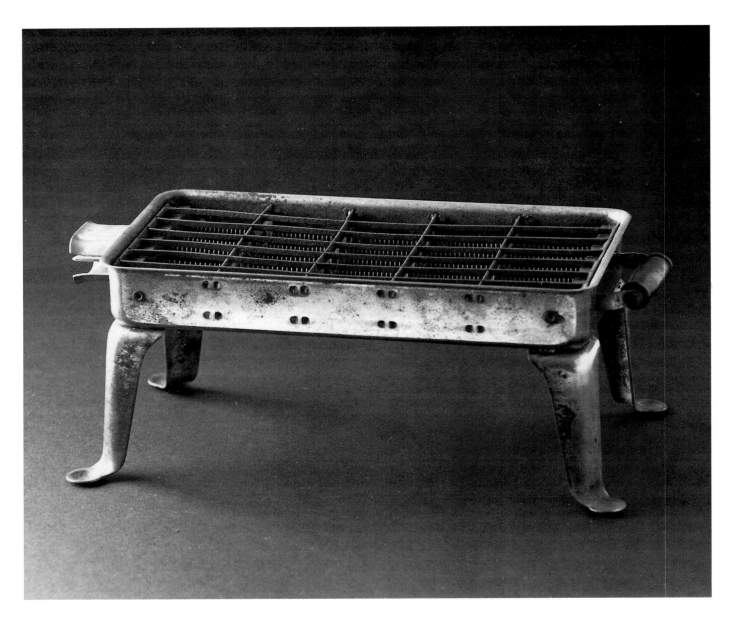

UNKNOWN, NOT MARKED

HOTPOINT TOASTER STOVE?

Rather cheaply made. Could also be in Combo category,
but no additional pots and pans found with it. Looks like
the Hotpoint Toaster Stove but no markings. If it is the
Hotpoint it sold for $4 when new.

TAMCO

TRIANGLE APPLIANCE MFG. CO. CHICAGO
115 VOLTS. 4.4 AMPS. TWO SLICES

Sturdy Flat Bed. The rotating basket absorbs a lot of heat leaving the toast heavily marked. Very difficult to remove toast without burned fingers.

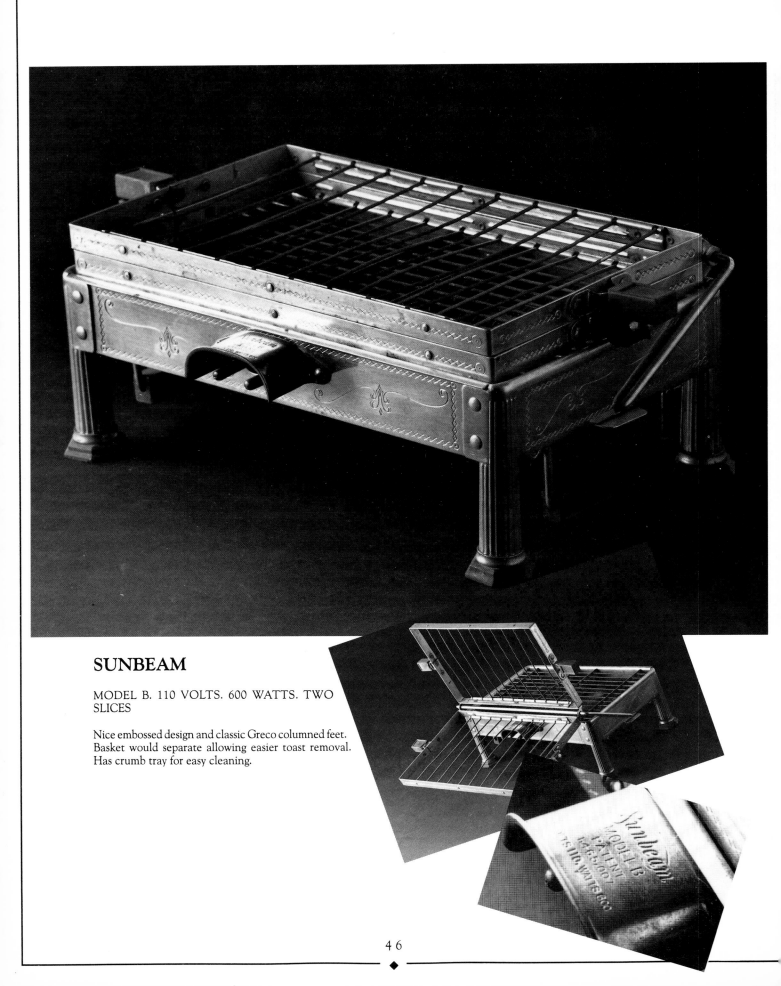

SUNBEAM

MODEL B. 110 VOLTS. 600 WATTS. TWO
SLICES

Nice embossed design and classic Greco columned feet.
Basket would separate allowing easier toast removal.
Has crumb tray for easy cleaning.

PROCTOR THERMOSTATIC TOASTER

PROCTOR & SCHWARTZ, INC. PHILADELPHIA
"YOU CANNOT BURN THE TOAST." 110 VOLTS. 550
WATTS. PATENTED JUNE 2, 1925

A lot of machinery to just make one slice.

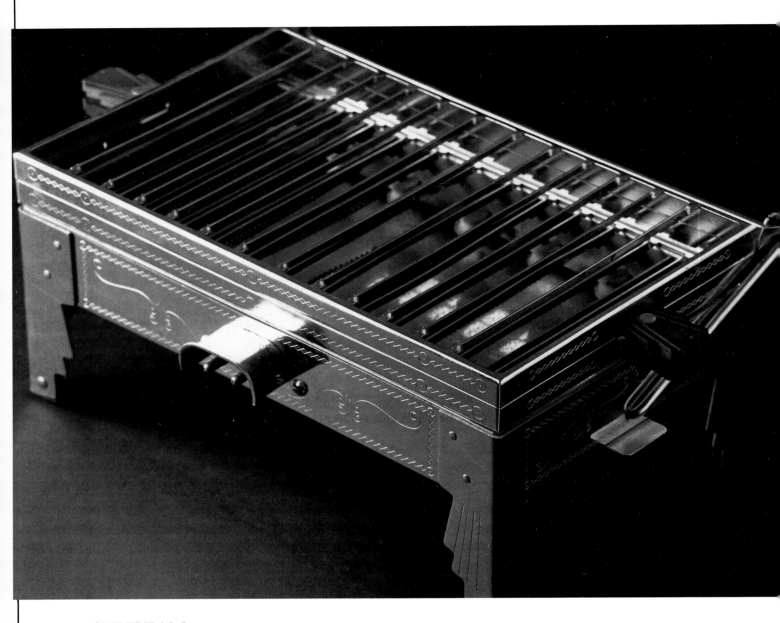

SUNBEAM

NO. 4. 110-120 VOLTS. 660 WATTS. PATENT NO.
1465007

Very similar to Model B in mechanics. Deco design with
newly designed feet and somewhat of a southwestern Native American motif, however unintentional. Very common at flea markets usually in good condition.

TURNERS
&
SWINGERS

Toast That Whirls Around

4

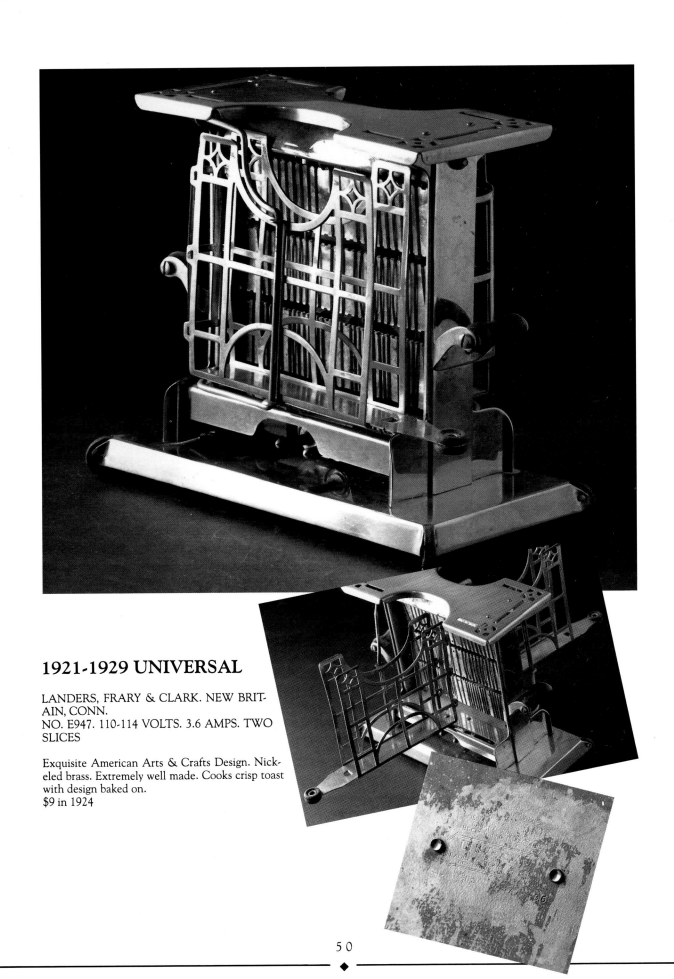

1921-1929 UNIVERSAL

LANDERS, FRARY & CLARK. NEW BRIT-
AIN, CONN.
NO. E947. 110-114 VOLTS. 3.6 AMPS. TWO
SLICES

Exquisite American Arts & Crafts Design. Nickeled brass. Extremely well made. Cooks crisp toast
with design baked on.
$9 in 1924

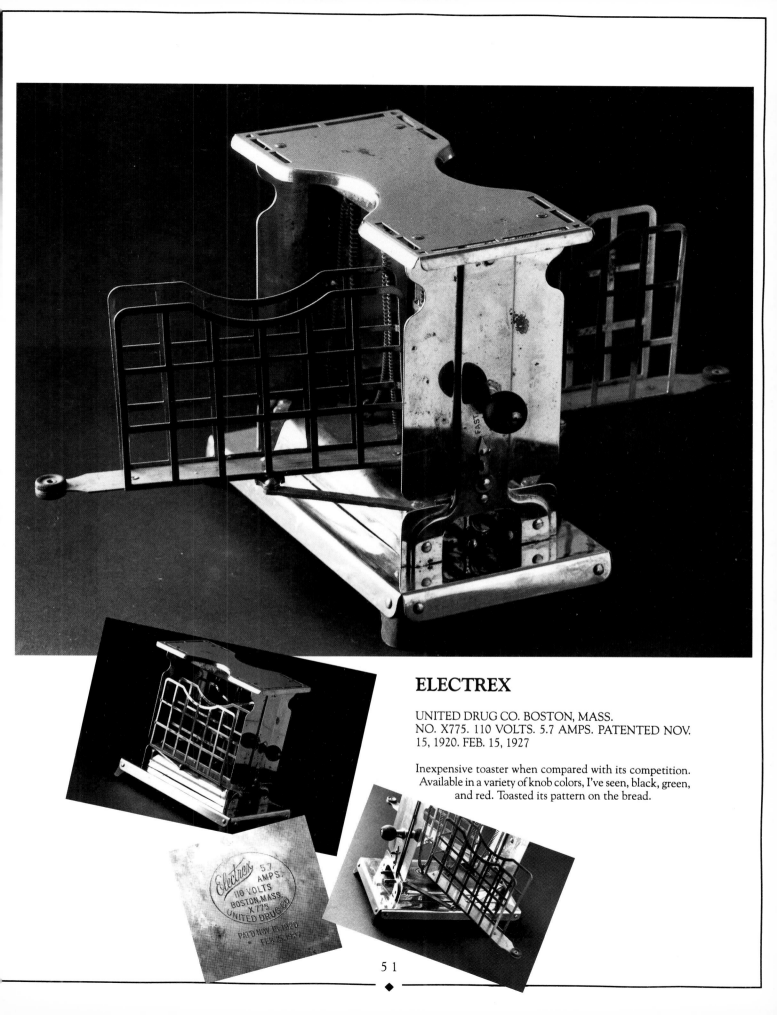

ELECTREX

UNITED DRUG CO. BOSTON, MASS.
NO. X775. 110 VOLTS. 5.7 AMPS. PATENTED NOV.
15, 1920. FEB. 15, 1927

Inexpensive toaster when compared with its competition.
Available in a variety of knob colors, I've seen, black, green,
and red. Toasted its pattern on the bread.

GOLD SEAL

GOLD SEAL ELECTRIC COMPANY.
CLEVELAND, OHIO.
NO. G-22381. TRADE MARK "QUALITY,
VALUE, SERVICE." 110 VOLTS. TWO
SLICES

Cheaply made. Basket design toasts on bread.

M-B MEANS BEST

MANNING BOWMAN & COMPANY.
MERIDAN, CONNECTICUT
NO. 1225. 110 VOLTS. 500 WATTS. PAT-
ENTED 5-25. TWO SLICES

Great wire work. Baskets hold bread securely with the help of eight curved springs, the whole basket turns over to toast the other side. The problem develops when you want to get the toast out. You must open the hot basket with your fingers freeing the toast and burning your pinkies for sure. Clumsy design, a real Rube Goldberger. Slight design toasted on the bread.

1925 ESTATE ELECTRIC TOASTER

THE ESTATE STOVE COMPANY.
HAMILTON, OHIO
NO. 177. 110 VOLTS. 5.5 AMPS. FOUR
SLICES

Here's a wacky one, you turn one door and they all turn around. It looks like an explosion in a toast factory. An earlier model, carrying a model number of #77 had wire doors and only one handle, but it worked the same way. Breakfast with this model was a real laugh.

1925-1930 STAR ELECTRIC TOASTER

FITZGERALD MFG. CO. TORRINGTON, CONN.
75000. 105-115 VOLTS. 550 WATTS. TWO SLICES

At least three variations made, with and without star cutouts, with black, red knobs, with and without handles. Little Pilgram Hat knobs get really hot and difficult to manipulate. Toasts a nice pattern on the bread. Crisp toast. Similar model made in 1923.

EXCELSIOR TWIN REVERSIBLE TOASTER

THE PERFECTION ELECTRIC PRODUCTS COM-
PANY. NEW WASHINGTON, OHIO
100-115 VOLTS. 4.7 WATTS. TWO SLICES

Twin baskets rotate as the crank is turned, turning the toast. If you crank fast enough it will
take off like a helicopter. Sturdy and fun to
play with. Toasts a nice pattern on the bread.
Another model labeled Excelsior Upright
Toaster was identical.

1929 UNIVERSAL

LANDERS, FRARY & CLARK. NEW BRITAIN, CONN.
NO. E9410. 108-116 VOLTS. 525 WATTS. TWO
SWINGING SLICES

One of the most elegant toaster designs ever made. Hand
sculpted molds were made to cast the liquid brass. The
ivory bakelite "earrings," buttons, and feet added to the
look of opulence while the basket delivered a beautiful
design on your morning toast. Each push button inde-
pendently tilted one basket down at a 45° angle turned
it over and lifted it back to face the heat. Truly a sight
to see. It's all done with six little levers hidden in the
base. Made to last a lifetime. There was another version No. E9411 which had a plain base.

SLIDERS
&
DRIVE THRU'S

Barn Doors and Endless Action

5

"TWIN OVEN"

MONTGOMERY WARD & CO. CHICAGO, ILLINOIS "SATISFACTION GUARANTEED OR YOUR MONEY BACK." 110-125 VOLTS. 660 WATTS. PATENTED SEPT. 4, 1923. TWO SLICES

This vertical drawer toaster carries no design on it anywhere—were the artists asleep or just cheap? You manually shove the drawer in and out checking on the doneness of your toast.

Courtesy of Joe Lukach

UNIVERSAL

LANDERS, FRARY & CLARK. NEW BRITAIN, CONN.
NO. E942. 106-114 VOLTS. 5 AMPS. PATENTED 1925.
ONE SLICE ONLY

A vertical drawer toaster in nickelplate. You pull the drawer
in and out to check the browning of the toast. Low bars on
top act as a warming rack.

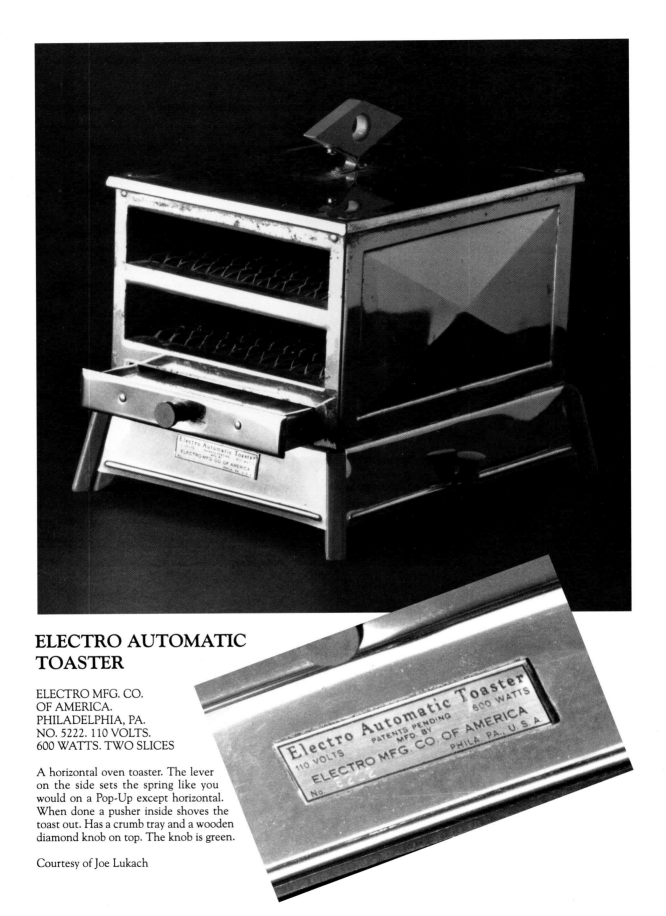

ELECTRO AUTOMATIC TOASTER

ELECTRO MFG. CO.
OF AMERICA.
PHILADELPHIA, PA.
NO. 5222. 110 VOLTS.
600 WATTS. TWO SLICES

A horizontal oven toaster. The lever
on the side sets the spring like you
would on a Pop-Up except horizontal.
When done a pusher inside shoves the
toast out. Has a crumb tray and a wooden
diamond knob on top. The knob is green.

Courtesy of Joe Lukach

1925-1930 UNIVERSAL

LANDERS, FRARY & CLARK. NEW BRITAIN, CONN. U.S.A.
NO. E9422. 108-116 VOLTS. 550 WATTS. "THE TRADE MARK KNOWN IN EVERY HOME." ONE SLICE ONLY

Elegant hot box. This model is nickel plated, others were chrome. Automatic action. It has a browning timer and a push down lever and a spring that slid the drawer out when done. Very well made, but a loner.

1930S COLEMAN TOASTER OVEN

WICHITA, KANS.

MODEL 2. A31. 115 VOLTS. 575 WATTS. PATENTED APRIL 29, 1930. TWO SLICE

Made by the famous lantern, stove, and camping gear maker. Pretty nice design for a bunch of outdoorsmen. The drawers slide out automatically when the toast is done. Crumb tray in bottom.

Courtesy of Joe Lukach

NO MARKINGS

IDENTICAL TO DOMINION,
TOAST-O-MATIC NO. 745

Well made slider. Bread is loaded in the top where it comes to rest on an angled ramp. There are two narrow doors that hold the bread in until it turns to toast. When done the timer signals the doors to open and the toast slides down the ramp onto the outer tray. Well, sometimes it does. Quite often the toast gets stuck and burns if you're not there to release it. A real great toaster even if it is quirky.

1938 SAMSON TRI-MATIC

SAMSON-UNITED CORP. ROCHESTER, N.Y. MADE IN U.S.A.
NO. 194. 115 VOLTS. 925 WATTS. PATENT NO. 2,059,440 AND 97,209. PATENTS PENDING 127. THREE SLICER

Very architectural toaster, reminds me of a bank building. Formal, but a "Lot-O-Gadgets" toaster. Push the lever on the side and the drawer slides in, this action also stretches the spring which will push the drawer out when the timer releases it. Whew! The timer control is on the back along with an on and off switch. There's a manual release next to the cocking lever.

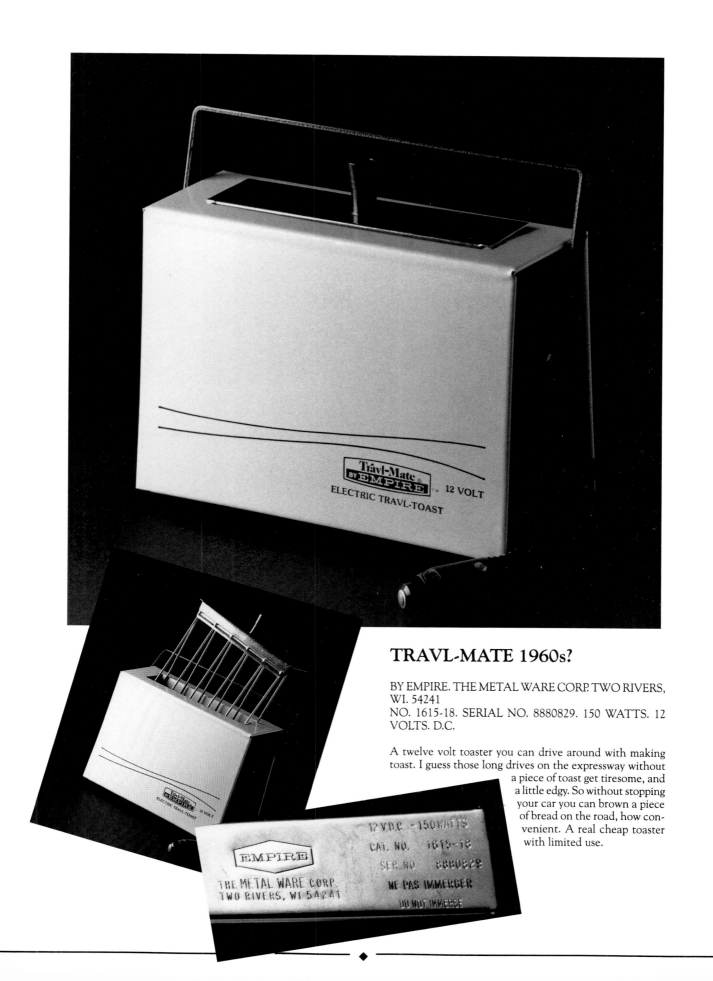

TRAVL-MATE 1960s?

BY EMPIRE. THE METAL WARE CORP. TWO RIVERS, WI. 54241
NO. 1615-18. SERIAL NO. 8880829. 150 WATTS. 12 VOLTS. D.C.

A twelve volt toaster you can drive around with making toast. I guess those long drives on the expressway without a piece of toast get tiresome, and a little edgy. So without stopping your car you can brown a piece of bread on the road, how convenient. A real cheap toaster with limited use.

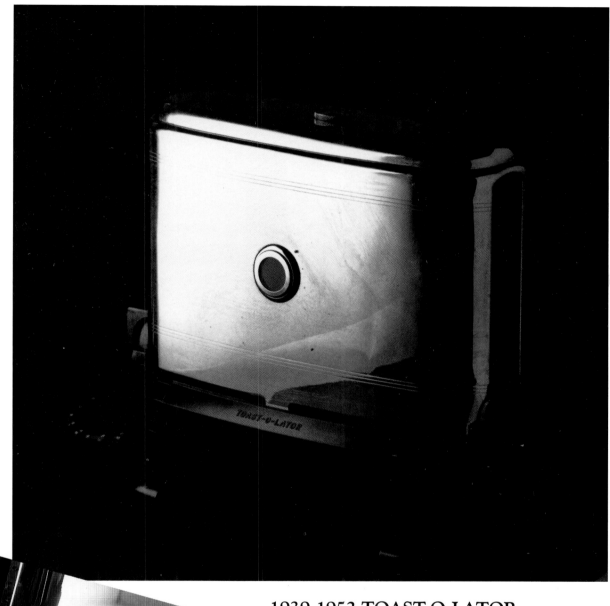

1939-1952 TOAST-O-LATOR

TOAST-O-LATOR COMPANY, INC. LONG ISLAND CITY, NEW YORK.
"THE CADILLAC OF TOASTERS." MODEL NO. H. SERIAL NO. 1146. 110-125 VOLTS. 600-825 WATTS. END LESS CAPACITY

This is the original Drive Thru Car Wash toaster. "Good bye bread, hello toast." Put a slice in one end and the conveyer system propels it past the heating element, it just keeps going and going. The mechanics are fascinating. Two saw-like metal strips move up and down as well as back and forth coaxing the bread thru the heated box. It's the most complicated toaster ever made. Three basic designs were made. A, B, and C were unique. A was squareish with no port hole. B was similar to the photo but with no port hole. C was like the photo and so was D,E,F,G,H,I, and J. The latter letters only stand for a change in year, not in design. It doesn't toast any better than most of its cheaper competitors but it sure is fun to play with. Kinda looks like a primitive diving helmet or 50s alien helmet.

TIPPERS

Toast Tips Out of A Hot Box

6

SUPER LECTRIC

SUPERIOR ELECTRIC
NO. 66. ONE SLICE

This is a cute little toaster. It is made adequately but with a
real quirky sense of design. Kind of like a joke toaster but
one that works. Has a coil element with what looks like
asbestos insulation.

Courtesy of Joe Lukach

1930s BERSTED

BERSTED MFG. CO. CHICAGO
115 VOLTS. 660 WATTS. ONE SLICE

Some models had timers and shut the heat down. Unusual design with an unpolished rectangular side panel bearing the embossed work. The wires making up the basket are very thin and seem fragile but they don't absorb much heat toasting the bread without much pattern. This example is in bad condition.

SUPER LECTRIC OVEN TOASTER

SUPERIOR ELECTRIC PRODUCTS
CORP. ST. LOUIS, MO.
NO. 77. 110 VOLTS. 500 WATTS. AC OR
DC. ONE SLICE

What a dog! This is a lousy toaster and cheaply
made. Just a hot box with a lever on the side,
which when pushed down tilted the toast up and
theoretically it slid out. It never does. The design
is nonexistent. It's not even dumb or bad design—
it's no design. Get the idea I don't think much of
this toaster? This company made many models that
were no design or they were like the #66 on an earlier page—so bad they created their own style.

UNKNOWN, NOT MARKED

A very intriguing little toaster. The side basket is cut and bent out of the same sheet metal as the frame. Makes a nice repeating design. The levers on the ends tilt the toast up and against the angled basket where you pluck it out. Classy base. The whole toaster is classy in a pedestrian way.

Courtesy of Joe Lukach

MAJESTIC AUTO-MATIC TOASTER

MAJESTIC ELECTRIC APPLIANCE CO.,
INC. SAN FRANCISCO. KANSAS CITY.
PHILADELPHIA
TYPE 66 T. 110 VOLTS. 660 WATTS. T-6974.
TWO SLICES

Elegant in a klunky way. Piercing is straight forward and American Arts & Crafts in design. The
front hanging earring is a door pull down that tips
the toast out of the box. Its design is very clean.
Partially closed top produces moist toast.

Courtesy of Joe Lukach

UNKNOWN, NOT MARKED

Boring. The lever on the side winds the timer when rotated. Light and dark setting on back side.

STAR RITE AUTOMATIC TOASTER

THE FITZGERALD MFG. CO. TORRINGTON
CATALOG 529 CP. 115 VOLTS. 880 WATTS. AC ONLY.

The locomotive design look. In line with the design concepts of the 30s. This one has a great base—it's a Buick bumper. Timer with dark, light setting. You'll find the same side panel design on another toaster in the Flopper section.

Courtesy of Joe Lukach

1930s UNIVERSAL

LANDERS, FRARY & CLARK. NEW BRITAIN, CONN.
NO. E2122F. 110-120 VOLTS. 800 WATTS. PATENT NO. 2088499. TWO SLICES.

Substantial and heavy. Well made. You tilt the door to get a gander at the toast. Has a timer and a bell but they are only reminders and don't shut off the heat or open the basket. Nice wire work and piercing.

UNIVERSAL

LANDERS, FRARY & CLARK. NEW
BRITAIN, CONN.
E7822F. 110-115 VOLTS. 800 WATTS.
2155852. TWO SLICES

Another locomotive type. Side panel cries for
some crest or some initials. American Arts &
Crafts piercing on skirt. Sports a timer and pops
open when done. Well made like most of the
LF&C products.

1930s HOTPOINT

GENERAL ELECTRIC APPLIANCE
COMPANY. CHICAGO, ILLINOIS.
115 VOLTS. 525 WATTS.

Automatic. Tilts the toast out of the toaster
when done. Timer has adjustment wheel that
has a range from "A" to "K." A to K? Crumb
tray. Often called the Gazelle by collectors, but
nowhere does Hotpoint call it that. A real beauty
of deco design and stateliness. Made like a tank
except for its side handles which break easily. The
plug shown was on the toaster when I got it, I don't
think it's the one that came with this model.

FLOPPERS

Toast Flops Out and Flips Over

7

1917-1924 TURNOVER TOASTER

WESTINGHOUSE ELECTRIC & MFG. CO.
PITTSBURGH
AB 3965. STYLE 231570. TWO SLICES

The first toaster to turn the toast over automatically. The turnover mechanism was a Copeman patent. It was just bent wires at the base of the toast that turned it over, but it was an elegant solution. Many companies tried to turn the toast without infringement on the Copeman patent, some inventing wild solutions to do what a few bent wires did. Has a ceramic element core which in later years became mica wrapped. White porcelain plug. Has a toast warming rack on top.

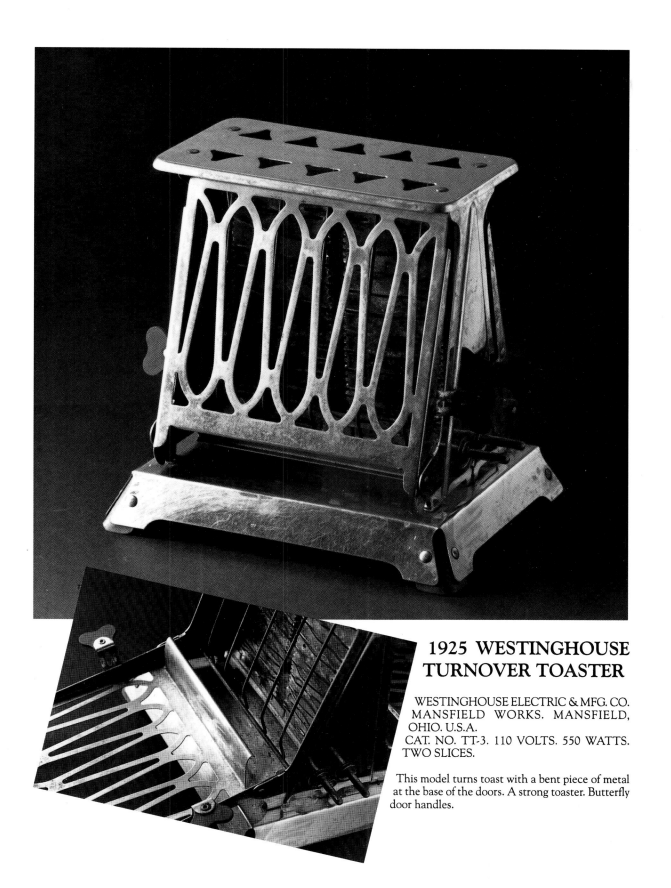

1925 WESTINGHOUSE TURNOVER TOASTER

WESTINGHOUSE ELECTRIC & MFG. CO.
MANSFIELD WORKS. MANSFIELD,
OHIO. U.S.A.
CAT. NO. TT-3. 110 VOLTS. 550 WATTS.
TWO SLICES.

This model turns toast with a bent piece of metal
at the base of the doors. A strong toaster. Butterfly
door handles.

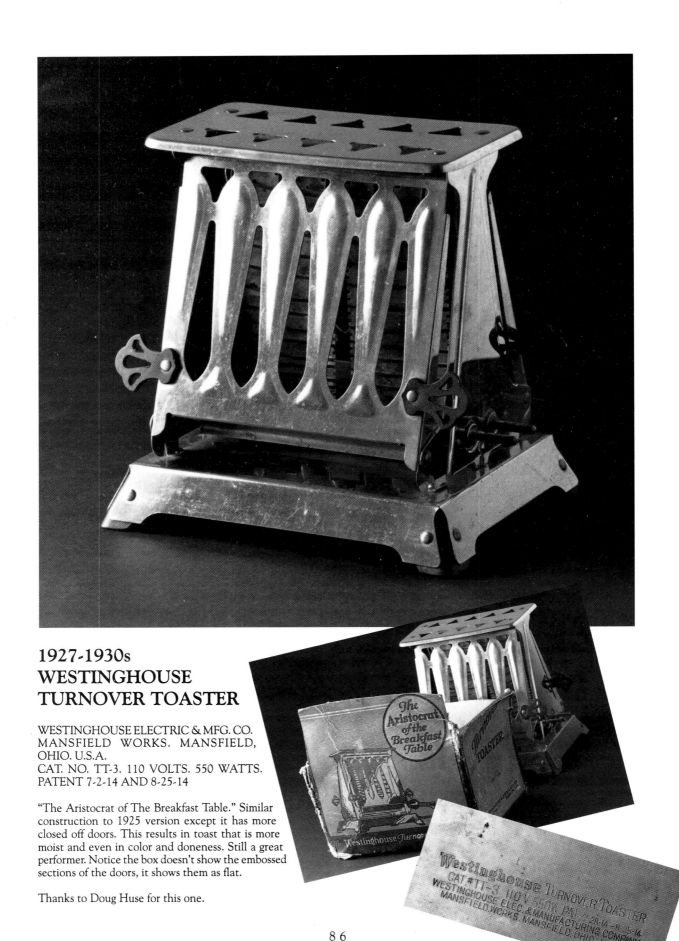

1927-1930s
WESTINGHOUSE
TURNOVER TOASTER

WESTINGHOUSE ELECTRIC & MFG. CO.
MANSFIELD WORKS. MANSFIELD,
OHIO. U.S.A.
CAT. NO. TT-3. 110 VOLTS. 550 WATTS.
PATENT 7-2-14 AND 8-25-14

"The Aristocrat of The Breakfast Table." Similar
construction to 1925 version except it has more
closed off doors. This results in toast that is more
moist and even in color and doneness. Still a great
performer. Notice the box doesn't show the embossed
sections of the doors, it shows them as flat.

Thanks to Doug Huse for this one.

ROYAL ROCHESTER

ROBESON ROCHESTER CORP. ROCHESTER, N.Y.
E6412. 110-120 VOLTS. 465 WATTS. TWO SLICES.

A fairly well made toaster but a little tinny. Tulip design pierced into doors. This design will be used on many Royal Rochester toasters.

HOTPOINT

EDISON ELECTRIC APPLIANCE CO.
CHICAGO. ONTARIO, CA.
CAT. 126T33.110 VOLTS. 625 WATTS.
PATENT APRIL 1, 1921, FEB. 22, 1910
AND JULY 28, 1911. TWO SLICES

Good looking toaster with nice pierced design
(which we will see later on another model).
Has a timer which rings a bell.

HOTPOINT RADIO TOGGLE TOASTER

EDISON ELECTRIC APPLIANCE CO.
CHICAGO. ONTARIO, CA.
CAT. 159T33.115 VOLTS. 660 WATTS.
PATENT APRIL 1, 1921, FEB. 22, 1910
AND JULY 28, 1911. TWO SLICES

Turns both sides of the toast at once, which
has its advantages as well as its disadvantages.
Turn the knob on the side and both doors flop
down at the same time. The knob looks like a
refugee from a radio parts store. Has a timer, nice
embossing, and the same door design as No.
126T33

EDISON ELECTRIC
MANUFACTURING CO.

EDISON ELECTRIC APPLIANCE CO. CHICAGO.
ONTARIO, CAL.
CAT. NO. 816T226. 110 VOLTS. 625 WATTS. TWO
SILCES

This one looks just like a Hotpoint and is. Very nice pierced
doors with engraving in the center. Pierced handles should
make them cooler, but not so you could tell the difference.
Good toaster.

HOTPOINT

EDISON ELECTRIC APPLIANCE CO. A GENERAL
ELECTRIC ORGANIZATION. CHICAGO, ONTARIO,
CAL.
CAT. NO. 157126. 115 VOLTS. TWO SLICES

Same door design as No.816T226, and everything else,
except this one is radio controlled. Well... its got the Radio
Knob. And that's like the No.159T33. And its made by
Hotpoint, Edison, and GE? Woof. Acts like a business deal
not a toaster.

UNKNOWN, NOT MARKED

Medieval war visor. This boy is cheap but rugged. It has fold marks on the radius of the legs indicating cheap metal drawing work. Thin but very strong steel body. It has a toast turning feature, cut down poker chips for handles, and a new cord. It's a wounded warrior. No nonsense.

UNKNOWN, NOT MARKED

TWO SLICES

Aluminum toaster. No design, no fun, just toast the toast.
Body of the toaster heated up fast but held heat poorly.
Maybe made right after WW2 or just made inexpensively,
it's hard to know.

UNKNOWN, NOT MARKED

Another Medieval warrior. Straight ahead toaster no frills. Real cheap element insulation and mechanical design. This example is rusty but it shows traces of green paint on the base. Wooden knobs.

UNKNOWN, NOT MARKED

Another rugged unknown toaster. Same toaster with different doors as the one on previous page. Same traces of green paint on base.

UNKNOWN, NOT MARKED

Another aluminum job but this one's painted light olive green. I wouldn't have picked that color. Cheap. How it lasted this long being so cheap will remain a mystery. Attempted deco design on ends.

Courtesy of Joe Lukach

HOLD HEET

RUSSELL ELECTRIC CO. CHICAGO
110 VOLTS. 4 AMPS. TWO SLICES

Great little logo of a man wearing a floppy hat and old shoes holding a circular sign with the name of the toaster on it. How the advertising people thought this was appealing to Mrs. homemaker is lost in history. This is a good substantial toaster with no particular oustanding features.

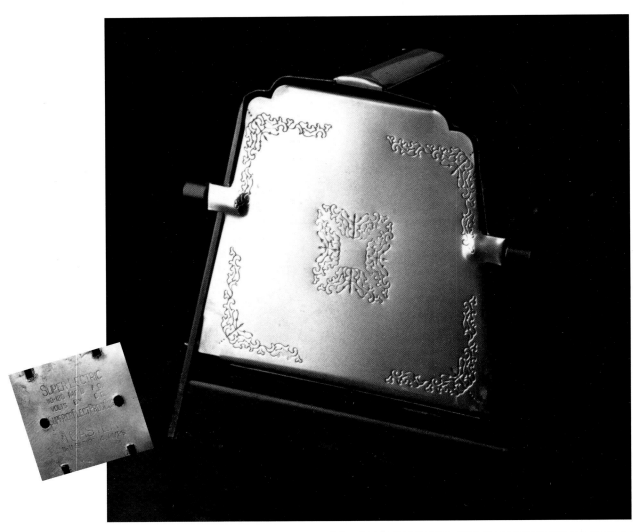

SUPER LECTRIC

SUPERIOR ELECTRIC PRODUCTS CO.
NO. H SERIES. 110-120 VOLTS. 4 AMPS.
AC OF DC. TWO SLICES.

Nice filigree stamping on the doors and a fairly elegant toaster for a cheapie. Nothing special here,
what you see is what you get. This basic design would
carry a variety of door treatments.

SUPER LECTRIC

SUPERIOR ELECTRIC CORP.
NO. 11 SERIES (COULD BE "H" SERIES) 110-
120 VOLTS. 4 AMPS. AC OR DC.

More deco door design than its brother above. The
same toaster in every other way.

THERM-A-HOT REVERSO

KNAPP-MONARCH CO. BELLVILLE, ILL. U.S.A.
110 VOLTS. 550 WATTS. PATENT NOs. 80 348-1,756. 784

Little compact toaster. Not a bad design, again, nothing special. The handles look to be made of poker chips, this is the second one I have that has had this done to it. It seems to solve the problem of no handles in a pinch. This was the second toaster I bought.

BEE-VAC

BIRTMAN ELECTRIC COMPANY. CHICAGO.
110-120 VOLTS. 625 WATTS AT 115 VOLTS. TWO SLICES.

This is a majestic toaster, big in size, bold in its design, but very light in weight. It commands the table it sits on. Could accommodate the largest loaf size with no problem. Very sturdy. Another Medieval Helm. Interesting turnover mechanism, a rod pulls the vertical supports forward and turns the toast

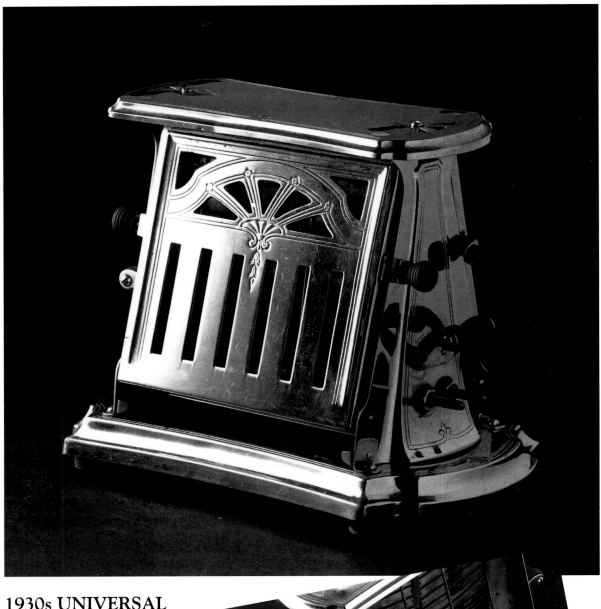

1930s UNIVERSAL

LANDERS, FRARY & CLARK. NEW BRIT-
AIN, CONN.
NO. E7712. 110-120 VOLTS. 625 WATTS.
TWO SLICES.

Beautifully drawn and sculpted sides. Has black
casein handles, which were also available in ivory
casein. Well made with great attention to detail,
note the excellent stamping work and piercing.
The base shows classic influences. Another winner from Universal.
$7.50 in 1932

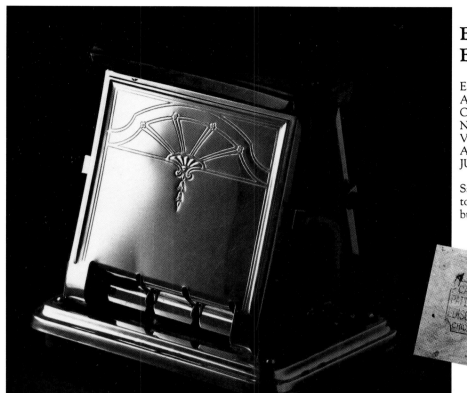

EDISON
ELECTRIC

EDISON ELECTRIC APPLI-
ANCE CO. INC. CHICAGO.
ONTARIO, CAL.
NO. E912A. 110-120
VOLTS. 625 WATTS. PAT.
APR. 1, 1924. FEB. 22, 1910.
JULY 28, 1914. TWO SLICES

Same door design as the
toaster on the previous page
but without the piercing.

BRUST-HARIS
MFG. CO. CHI-
CAGO, ILL.

A real cheapie. Thin stamped
metal with few toast support
wires. A design that is bad but
shows some thought. Deco in
spirit.

Courtesy of Joe Lukach

SECURITY

SECURITY ELECTRIC MFG. CO. CHICAGO,
U.S.A.
NO. 220. 110 VOLTS. 500 WATTS. TWO SLICES.

Well made with a heavy duty element and support.
Rather pedestrian design.

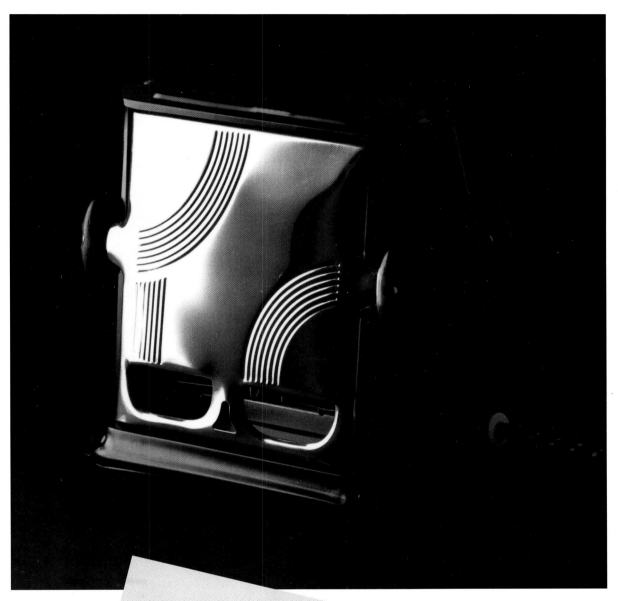

SON-CHIEF

SON-CHIEF ELECTRIC INC. WINSTED, CONN. U.S.A.
SERIES 680. 115 WATTS. 550 WATTS. TWO SLICES.

Just one in a long series this company made of cheap toasters. Made many door styles on this same frame. Wooden knobs also varied in color from black to varnished wood to white. A tin toaster. Maybe the word started here.

CORONET

CONNECTICUT APPLIANCE CO.
WINSTED, CONN. U.S.A.
SERIES 680. 115 VOLTS. 550 WATTS.
TWO SLICES.

Same toaster as the previous page,
Sun-Chief 680, just different doors.

UNKNOWN, NOT
MARKED

Aluminum toaster. Cheap.

THERMAX

LANDERS, FRARY & CLARK. NEW BRITAIN, CONN.

NO. E3342. 117-125 VOLTS. 625 WATTS. PATENTED JULY 28, 1914. TWO SLICES.

Strong well made toaster with American Arts & Crafts design piercing on doors. Turned wooden feet.

UNKNOWN, NOT MARKED

Brass toaster, not chromed, with some kind of clear coating over it, a varnish maybe. Two slices.

FULL VISION

CAT. NO. 20. 115 VOLTS.
450 WATTS. PATENT
1,765,784. TWO SLICES

No mention of maker's name
on the toaster. There is an "M"
in a square that looks like a
logo, maybe. The so called
advantage, the full vision as-
pect, is no advantage at all because you can only see the side
of the bread that is *not* toasting. If you can only see the
non-toasting side then you
can't know when to turn the
toast over any better with this
toaster than with a solid door
toaster. Inexpensively made.

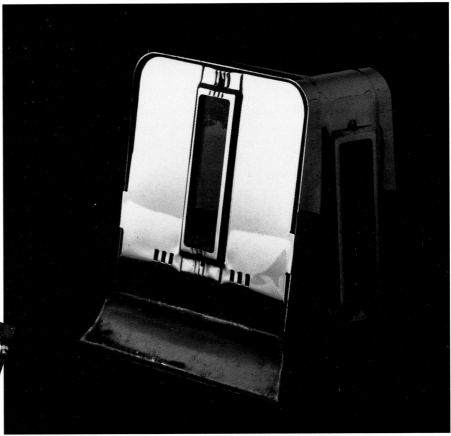

DEPENDABLE DOMINO DEVICES

DOMINION ELECTRIC
MFG. CO. MINNEAPOLIS,
MINN.
STYLE 48. 120 VOLTS. 550
WATTS. PATENT NO.
1,105,230. TWO SLICES.

Big toaster but light weight.
Notice door design will be very
similar on the next three pages
of toasters.
$4 in 1932

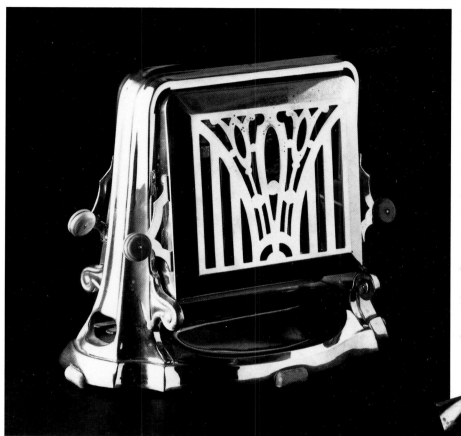

ROYAL ROCHESTER

ROBESON ROCHESTER CORPORATION. ROCH-ESTER, N.Y. NO. E6410. A-29. 110 VOLTS. 425 WATTS. TWO SLICES.

Extraordinary sculptural design, a piece of the metalsmiths art. Has the feeling of a sleek locomotive with its protruding cow catcher and smooth lines. The hinges are pure sculpture. Polished armor at the height of its development. White casein or bakelite handles and feet. Similar door piercing as the previous Domino and the Royal Rochester below.

Courtesy of Joe Lukach

ROYAL ROCHESTER

ROBESON ROCHESTER CORPORATION. ROCH-ESTER, N.Y. NO. 13300. D-33. 110-120 VOLTS. 500 WATTS. TWO SLICES.

Similar door design as previous two toasters. Not nearly the quality of the Royal Rochester that it shares its door with. A good solid inexpensive toaster though.

STEELCRAFT

115 VOLTS. 550 WATTS. TWO SLICES.

Explosion in a coat hanger factory. Came in a variety of colors. The feet are turned and painted wood. Just the bare minimum to get by. But for what it is, it has a certain style.

Courtesy of Joe Lukach

HEATMASTER

CATALOG 360-1973. 110-120 VOLTS.
500 WATTS. AC ONLY. TWO SLICES.

Timer thermostat shut heat off when done.
Heavily made base. Another candidate for rail-
road duty. Wooden knobs. Heatmaster was a
brand name of Sears & Roebuck.

GENERAL ELECTRIC

BRIDGEPORT, CONN.
ONTARIO, CALIF.
NO. 119T46. 115 VOLTS.
450 WATTS. TWO SLICES.

"So it's like I was sayin' we stamp a spider web on the doors, it'll be all the rage!" How did some designer convince the company to make this one?

UNIVERSAL

LANDERS, FRARY & CLARK. NEW BRITAIN, CONN. U.S.A.
NO. E8612. 110-120 VOLTS.
625 WATTS. TWO SLICES.

A rather poor example of design for Universal.

UNKNOWN

BUTLER BROTHERS?
MARKED WITH "N"
AND LIGHTNING
BOLT
CAT. 494A. 110-120
VOLTS. 500 WATTS.

Long tray like base with
wooden ends and knobs.
Real basic toaster.

SUPER STAR

NEW YORK, N.Y.
MADE IN U.S.A.
115 VOLTS. 500
WATTS.

Like German armor and
shield. Nice flaring base.
Wooden knobs.

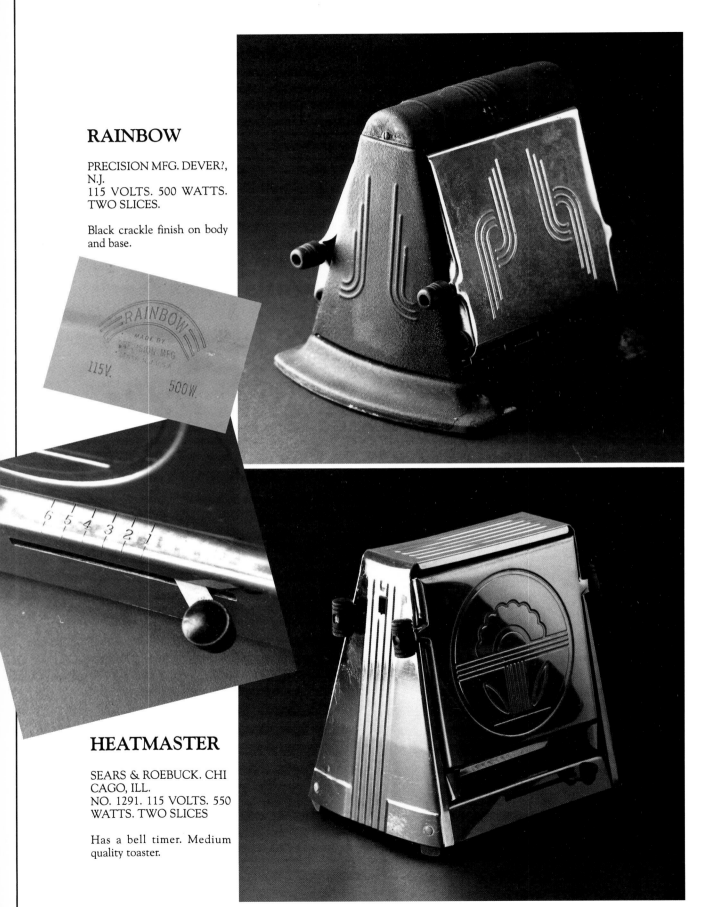

RAINBOW

PRECISION MFG. DEVER?, N.J.
115 VOLTS. 500 WATTS. TWO SLICES.

Black crackle finish on body and base.

HEATMASTER

SEARS & ROEBUCK. CHICAGO, ILL.
NO. 1291. 115 VOLTS. 550 WATTS. TWO SLICES

Has a bell timer. Medium quality toaster.

WESTINGHOUSE

MANSFIELD, OHIO
CAT. NO. TL-14. 115
VOLTS. 460 WATTS.
PATENT 2083518. TWO
SLICES

An understated design with
style and reserve. Cleanly
made with no nonsense.

STERLING

ANOTHER HANDY HOT
PRODUCT. CHICAGO
ELECTRIC MFG. CO.
TYPE AEUF. 110-120
VOLTS. 500 WATTS.
PATENT NO. 1,987,356.

The next five toasters are a
family using many of the same
parts to build different designs.
Inexpensively made but a case
of a good designer working at
a low cost company.

VICTORY
BRAND

A HANDY HOT PROD-
UCT. CHICAGO ELECTRIC
MFG. CO. CHICAGO, ILL.
TYPE AEU. 110-120 VOLTS.
500 WATTS. PATENT
83830

Deco design owing much to
southwestern Native American designs. Part of the five
toaster group.

VICTORY
BRAND

A HANDY HOT PROD-
UCT. CHICAGO ELECTRIC
MFG. CO. CHICAGO, ILL.
TYPE AEUA. 110-115
VOLTS. 500 WATTS.
PATENT NO. 89638

Another of the Handy Hot
family in this section. All are
good Deco designs. Notice the
handles are like others. Reminds me of a skyscraper.

1935 HANDY HOT

CHICAGO ELECTRIC
MFG. CO.
TYPE AEUB. 110-115
VOLTS. 500 WATTS. TWO
SLICES.

Now here's a locomotive if
ever I've seen one. Very stylish Deco design. Cheaply
made.

VICTORY BRAND

ANOTHER HANDY HOT
PRODUCT. CHICAGO
ELECTRIC MFG. CO.
TYPE AEU. 105-115 VOLTS.
500 WATTS. TWO SLICES.

The last grouping in this family of similar designs. Look at
the handles. Also reminiscent
of a much older toaster in its
door design—the Turnover
toasters by Westinghouse.
This group is a very nice design group albeit cheap.

MONTGOMERY WARD U.S.A.

CATALOG NO. 5254. 115 VOLTS. 450 WATTS. TWO SLICES.

Another shield and armor toaster. Inexpensive. Wooden handles.

HANDY HOT

CHICAGO ELECTRIC MFG. CO.
CAT. NO. 5902. 115 VOLTS. 400 WATTS. AC OR DC. PATENT NO. 1987356-2177177. TWO SLICES.

A Handy Hot but in a different design family than the ones on the previous pages. Armor like.

DOMINION

DOMINION ELECTRIC
MFG. CO. MANSFIELD,
OHIO.
STYLE 364. 110-120 VOLTS.
550 WATTS. TWO SLICES.

Wheat pattern on doors. This
toaster comes apart for easy
cleaning.

CHALLENGE

NO. E10552. CAT. S-76. 110
VOLTS.

A Deco armored Knight. The
wire on the base of this toaster
is not stock.

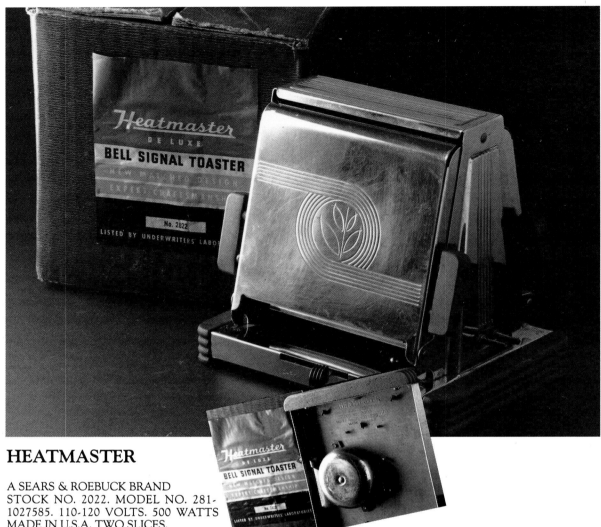

HEATMASTER

A SEARS & ROEBUCK BRAND
STOCK NO. 2022. MODEL NO. 281-
1027585. 110-120 VOLTS. 500 WATTS
MADE IN U.S.A. TWO SLICES.

Lack luster toaster. One of the few in boxes I
have. Has a bell timer. Wooden handles
and base ends.

WESTINGHOUSE
TURNOVER TOASTER

WESTINGHOUSE ELEC. & MANUFACTURING
COMPANY. MANSFIELD WORKS. MANSFIELD,
OHIO.
CAT. TT-C-94. 115 VOLTS. 550 WATTS. PAT. 7-28-
14 AND 8-25-14. TWO SLICES.

Trying to be a Deco toaster but in work clothes. This
door design will be seen later on another toaster.
Well made.

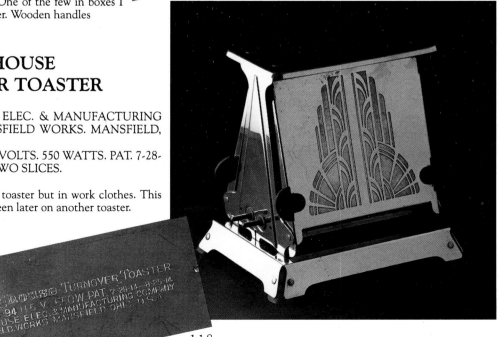

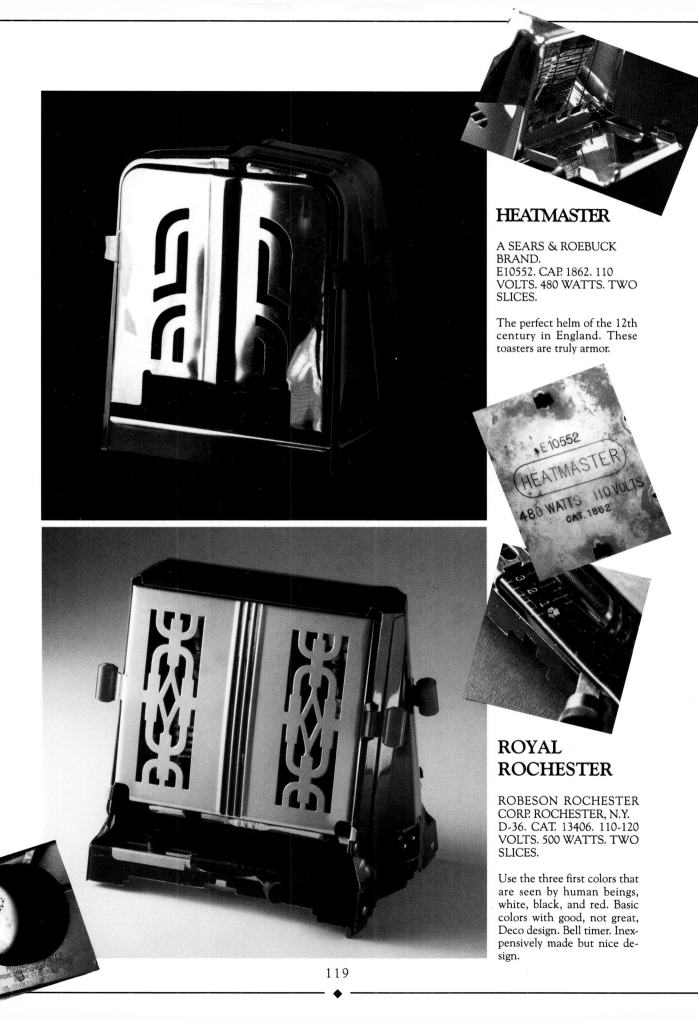

HEATMASTER

A SEARS & ROEBUCK
BRAND.
E10552. CAP. 1862. 110
VOLTS. 480 WATTS. TWO
SLICES.

The perfect helm of the 12th
century in England. These
toasters are truly armor.

ROYAL
ROCHESTER

ROBESON ROCHESTER
CORP. ROCHESTER, N.Y.
D-36. CAT. 13406. 110-120
VOLTS. 500 WATTS. TWO
SLICES.

Use the three first colors that
are seen by human beings,
white, black, and red. Basic
colors with good, not great,
Deco design. Bell timer. Inexpensively made but nice design.

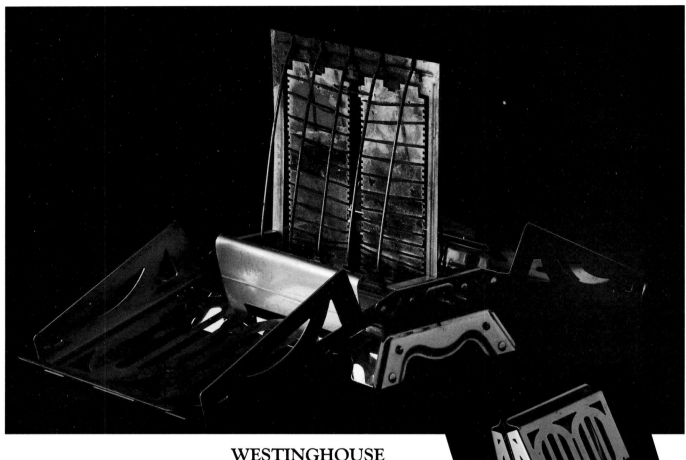

WESTINGHOUSE

TURNOVER TOASTER. WESTINGHOUSE
ELEC. & MANUFACTURING COMPANY.
MANSFIELD WORKS. MANSFIELD,
OHIO. U.S.A. TWO SLICES.
CAT. # TAC-3. 110 VOLTS. 550 WATTS. PAT.
NO. 7-28-14 — 8-25-14. TWO SLICES.

A most unusual turnover mechanism. Thank you Mr.
Goldberg. Strange off the wall engineering, especially
for Westinghouse.

KWIK-WAY

KWIK-WAY COMPANY. ST.
LOUIS. U.S.A.
CAT. NO. 21404. 115 VOLTS. 400
WATTS. TWO SLICES.

A mechanized flopper. Turn the
handle and both doors open at the
same time. Note mechanism in inte-
rior shot. Brown painted base. Unusual door engraving of a swan on
the water. Lightweight.

FOSTORIA

BERSTED MFG. CO.
FOSTORIA, O.
MODEL NO. 72. 115
VOLTS. 400 WATTS. TWO
SLICES.

Clean design. Wide base adds
stability and strength. Attrac-
tive.

MIRACLE

MIRACLE ELECTRIC CO.
CHICAGO 3, ILLINOIS.
CAT. NO. 210. 115 VOLTS.
400 WATTS. TWO SLICES.

Not much design. I've seen an
English model with this same
design. Cheap.

UNKNOWN, NOT MARKED

TWO SLICES

This is a striking toaster design. Its three quarter view is almost identical to the Chicago Picasso sculpture in the Daley Center. The angular lines and red knobs combine with the black body to set off the wheat design on the doors. It's one great looking toaster.

MERIT MADE

MERIT MADE. BUFFALO, N.Y.
MODEL-Z. 115 VOLTS. 375 WATTS. SERIAL NO. 323145-?

A mechanized flopper. Push the button and both sides flop open. They close automatically with a spring that pulls them together. Unique round style. Aluminum doors on this model.

1938 SUPERIOR ELECTRIC

SUPERIOR ELECTRIC PRODUCTS CORP. ST. LOUIS, MO.
66 SERIES. 110-120 VOLTS. 3.5 AMPS. AC OR DC. TWO SLICES

Excellent Deco design. Buck Rogers handles of red bakelite and chromed steel discs and heavy wire base. Well made. There was a 4 slice version as well as a more pedestrian style model that had wooden handles and a flat base.

RED SEAL

RED SEAL APPLIANCE
CO. ROCHESTER, N.Y.
MADE IN U.S.A.
NO. 7052. 115 VOLTS. 425
WATTS. PATENT NOs.
2,008,799 91180. 88. TWO
SLICES.

Well made toaster with a timer
and bell. The door piercing is
the same as the next toaster
on the next page.

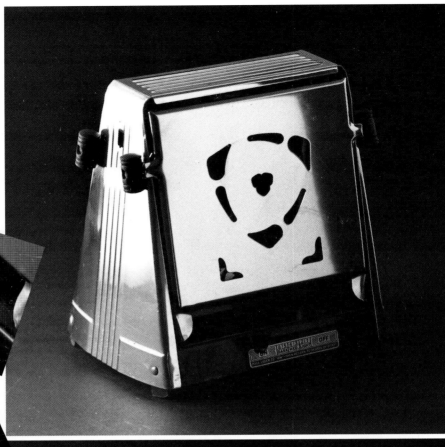

BASE MISSING, NO INFORMATION

PROBABLY RED SEAL?
TWO SLICES.

Well made. Note same door
piercing as previous toaster.
Nice sculpted sides and well
formed base. Handles are in
popular Deco design. Some
locomotive influence as well
as Buick fender influence.

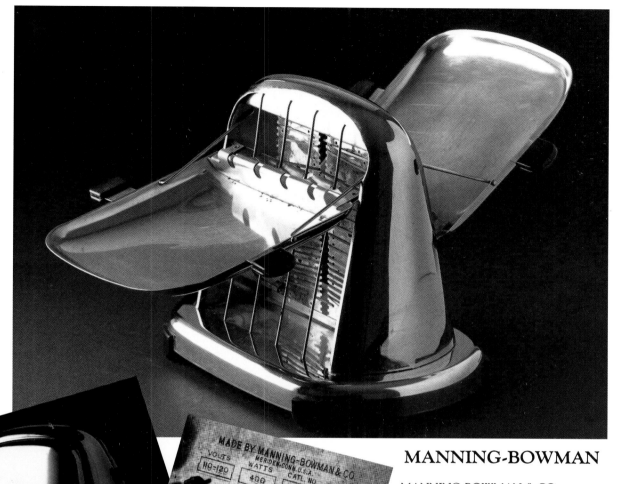

MANNING-BOWMAN

MANNING-BOWMAN & CO.
MERIDAN, CONN.
CAT. NO. 98. SERIAL NO. 6-50. 110-120
VOLTS. 400 WATTS. PATENT NO. 2477814.
TWO SLICES.

An early version of the Sikorsky single rotor helicopter. This boy looks like it's gonna take off. Unusual toast turning method. It starts to open like a normal flopper then the door pivots and the bottom rides up on vertical rods turning the door to horizontal and flipping the toast. Reverse the action to resume toasting the new side. A real joy to watch, it makes you laugh. One of the more difficult toast turning mechanisms to work smoothly. Must be a design made to avoid a patent infringement or a designer gone wild.

THE JUNIOR TOASTER

RIVERSIDE MANUFACTURING CO. YPSILANTI, MICHIGAN.
MODEL 1002. 110 VOLTS. 550 WATTS. TWO SLICES.

Buck Rogers must have made toast on this one. Great futuristic design and, like so often, cheaply made. Some versions are unmarked. Aluminum with crinkle finish black base.

UNKNOWN "BLACK WATER FALL"

Exquisite design with the sides looking like a rushing waterfall of turbulent froth. Nice metal drawing work as well as molding on the base. One classy toaster.

Courtesy of Joe Lukach

FOSTORIA

BERSTED MFG. CO. FOSTORIA, O. MODEL NO. 60. 115 VOLTS. 750 WATTS. FOUR SLICES.

Tinny four slicer. Nicely designed handles and stamping on door.

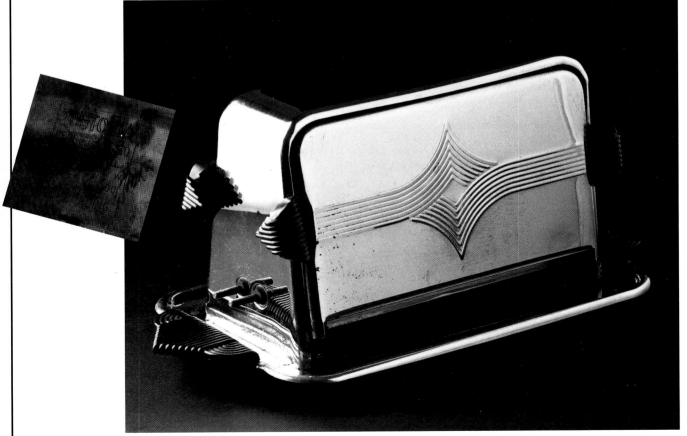

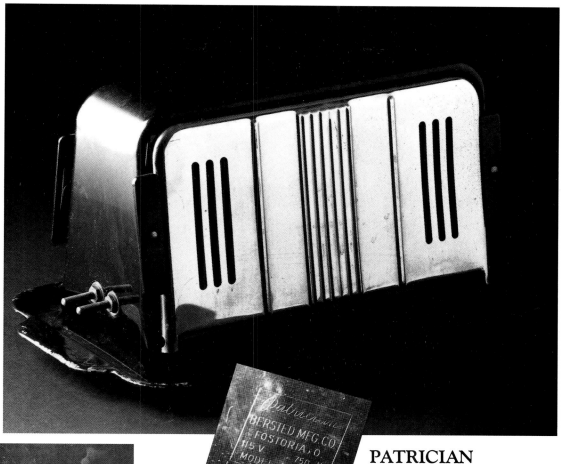

PATRICIAN

BERSTED MFG. CO. FOSTORIA, O.
MODEL NO. 65. 115 VOLTS. 750
WATTS. PATENT PENDING. FOUR
SLICES.

Another tinny toaster. Many of the home
four slicers seem to be cheaply made.
This one is no exception. No design to
speak of.

BUTLER BROTHERS

CAT. NO. 77R-3517. 110-120 VOLTS. 800
WATTS. AC OR DC. MARKED
WITH AN "N" AND A
LIGHTNING BOLT.
FOUR SLICES.

Another cheap four
slicer. Ivory bakelite
knobs and handles.

DROPPERS

Toast Falls Through A Trap Door

8

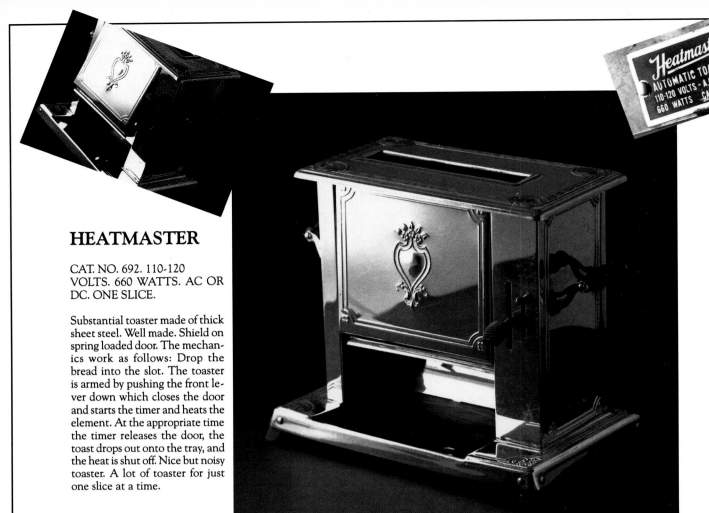

HEATMASTER

CAT. NO. 692. 110-120
VOLTS. 660 WATTS. AC OR
DC. ONE SLICE.

Substantial toaster made of thick
sheet steel. Well made. Shield on
spring loaded door. The mechanics work as follows: Drop the
bread into the slot. The toaster
is armed by pushing the front lever down which closes the door
and starts the timer and heats the
element. At the appropriate time
the timer releases the door, the
toast drops out onto the tray, and
the heat is shut off. Nice but noisy
toaster. A lot of toaster for just
one slice at a time.

L & H ELECTRIC AUTOMATIC TOASTER

J. LINDEMANN &
HOVERSON CO. MILWAU-
KEE, WISCONSIN
MODEL NO. 205. 110-120
VOLTS. 660 WATTS. TWO
SLICES.

All the Droppers seem to be very
well made and this one is also.
Here's the loading sequence:
Open the top, drop two slices in,
close the top, push the side lever
down, sit around reading the paper listening to the timer, times up,
the timer releases the trap doors
and the toast drops out, butter the
toast, enjoy. Yeow! This model has
a manual release, as well as a on/
off switch, lots of buttons! Another model has a top door that
has no holes in it.

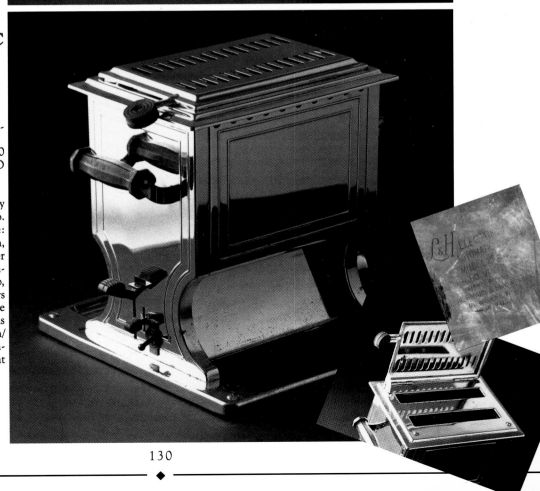

UNIVERSAL

LANDERS, FRARY & CLARK. NEW BRITAIN, CONN.
MODEL E7732. 108-115 VOLTS. 660 WATTS. DES. 87297. TWO SLICES.

A real dumb, well made, Dropper. Built like a tank. Here's the loading sequence: If the toaster is closed open it by pushing the side release button. The heavy door falls open and you load it with two slices. Push the door up to close and hit the timer, now the toast is cooking. When it's done the timer releases the door and it falls open delivering the done toast. A big, heavy, gawky toaster. There is a knob on the front door which is missing from this example. Toasts some basket marks on the toast.

1940s DELTA POP DOWN AUTOMATIC TOASTER

DELTA MANUFACTURING CORPORATION. PHILA., PENN.
MODEL NO. 280. 110-120 VOLTS. 940 WATTS. AC OR DC. TWO SLICES.

Another heavy duty model. It was also made in aluminum and in colors as well as the chrome job shown. This is how it works: Drop two slices into the top slots. Set the timer. Push down the handle to arm the doors, start the timer and turn the heat on. When done the timer releases the trap doors and the toast drops out onto the tray.

COMBOS

Higgledy-Piggledy...Hodgepodge

9

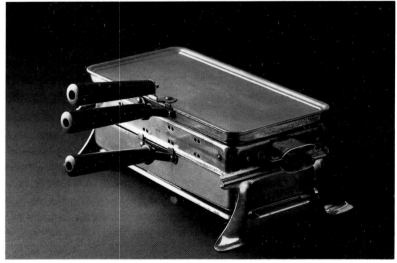

ARMSTRONG
PERC-O-TOASTER

ARMSTRONG ELECTRIC & MFG. CORP'N.
HUNTINGTON, W. VA.
MODEL PT. 110 VOLTS. 440 WATTS. 575
WATTS. ONE SLICE.

Early combo toaster and coffee percolator also had an optional waffle attachment which sold for $3.50. Sturdy. Has two sockets feeding current to the toaster and the percolator independently, hence the two wattage ratings. The handle is as found and is not stock.
$11.85 IN 1918.

EL GRILLO

HOTPOINT ELECTRIC HEATING CO. CHI-CAGO. NEW YORK. ONTARIO CAL.
VANCOUVER, TORONTO.
110 VOLTS. 5.5 AMPS. DATE 04-13

One of the early toaster-stove-toasters. Cooks bacon, eggs, toast, and a variety of other foods. Great appliance for someone in a one room apartment with no kitchen. Well made.

STANDARD TABLE STOVE

STANDARD STAMPING CO. HUN-
TINGTON, W. VA.
NO. 8-A. 110 VOLTS. 600 WATTS.
PATENT APR. 23, '18

A more versatile model than on the previous page. It even poaches eggs. Heavy
duty model. Well made. Some models
are white enamel, some green.

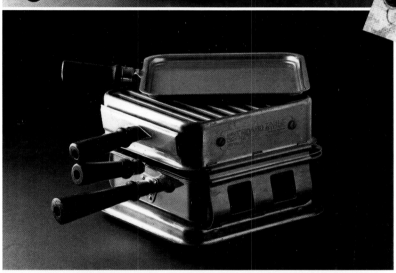

UNKNOWN, NOT MARKED

TWO SLICES. TWO POTS.

This combo model will service two coffee
makers as well as make toast. Was it for
restaurant use or just for a family who
loved coffee but weren't partial to toast? I
don't know. The one pictured is missing
its switches. I have seen another version
with toggle switches instead of the light
switch type. Cheap toaster but nice striped
design.

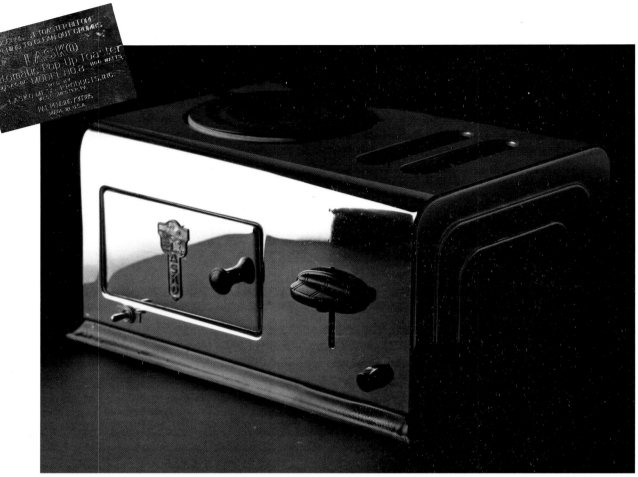

LASKO AUTOMATIC POP-UP TOASTER

LASKO METAL PRODUCTS INC. WEST CHESTER, PA.
MODEL NO. 8. 115 VOLTS. 1110 WATTS.
PAT. PENDING 730385. TWO SLICES.

Nicely made. This model also available in white enamel. Has a hot plate, a sort of oven and a toaster. Timer on the toaster.

40s-50s BREAKFASTER

CALKINS APPLIANCE CO. NILES, MICHIGAN. U.S.A.
MODEL T2. 115 VOLTS. 750 WATTS.
ONE SLICE.

Heavy cast aluminum and sheet aluminum. Well made and nicely finished casting. Has a hot plate and a toaster.

GENERAL ELECTRIC

BRIDGEPORT, CONN.
CAT. NO. 25T83. 120 VOLTS. 1200
WATTS. TWO SLICES.

Combination long slot, pop-up with a drawer
toaster. A real football.

POP-UPS

Spring Loaded

10

1926
TOASTMASTER

AUTOMATIC POP UP TOASTER. WATERS GENTER COMPANY. MINNEAPOLIS, MINN. MODEL 1A1. 110 VOLTS. 600 WATTS. #347025. ONE SLICE.

First automatic Pop-Up made for the home. Has a timer. Rugged construction, well made. Would set the standard for a quality toaster. Nickel plated at first then later models become chrome. $12.50 in 1926.

TOASTMASTER

WATERS GENTER COMPANY. MINNEAPOLIS, MINN. MODEL 1A3. NO. K-775115. 110 VOLTS. 600 WATTS. ONE SLICE.

The first toaster I ever collected. Also came in a two slice version. Well made.

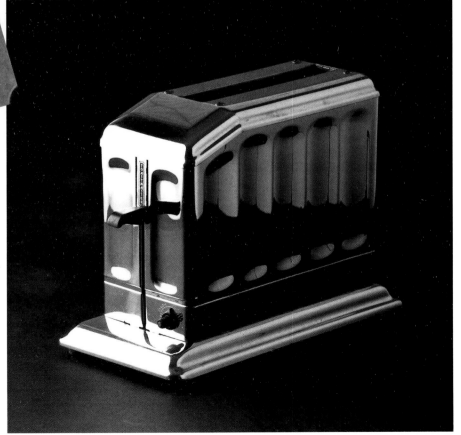

1939
TOASTMASTER

MC GRAW ELECTRIC
COMPANY. WATERS-
GENTER DIV. MPLS.,
MINN. U.S.A.
MODEL 1A4. NO. K-861651.
110 VOLTS. 600 WATTS.
ONE SLICE.

Another well made toaster by
the premier toaster maker in
the U.S.
$9.95 in 1939

TOASTMASTER

MC GRAW ELECTRIC
COMPANY. WATERS-
GENTER DIV. MPLS.,
MINN. U.S.A.
MODEL 1B5. NO. B-525947.
110 VOLTS. 10 AMPS. TWO
SLICES.

They just keep getting better.

TOASTMASTER

TOASTMASTER PROD-
UCTS DIVISION. MC
GRAW ELECTRIC CO.
ELGIN, ILL. U.S.A.
MODEL 1B8. NO. A-391425.
110 VOLTS. 10 AMPS. TWO
SLICES.

The locomotive look for
Toastmaster. Porthole design
on the side combined with
speed lines made this a modern looking toaster.

40s-50s
TOASTMASTER

TOASTMASTER PROD-
UCTS DIVISION. MC
GRAW ELECTRIC CO.
ELGIN, ILL. U.S.A.
MODEL 1B14. NO. A-
3266661. 110-120 VOLTS.
10.5 AMPS. TWO SLICES.

This model carried the squig-
gly line design on it sides that
was started by the Model
1B12. This design was used to
disguise the drawing marks left
when the metal was drawn
into shape. It is also the electrical symbol for a resistor.
Which is what the heating element is, a resistance wire.
This symbol will become syn-
onymous with toasters and of
course with Toastmaster in
particular.
$21.50 in 1950

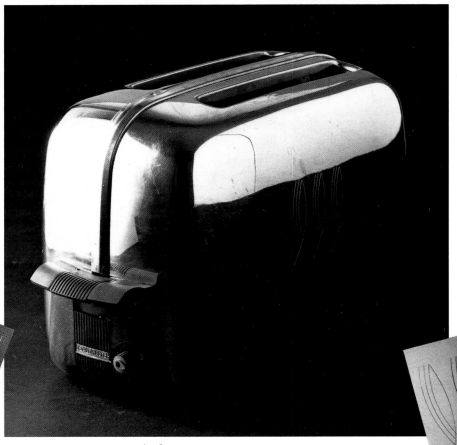

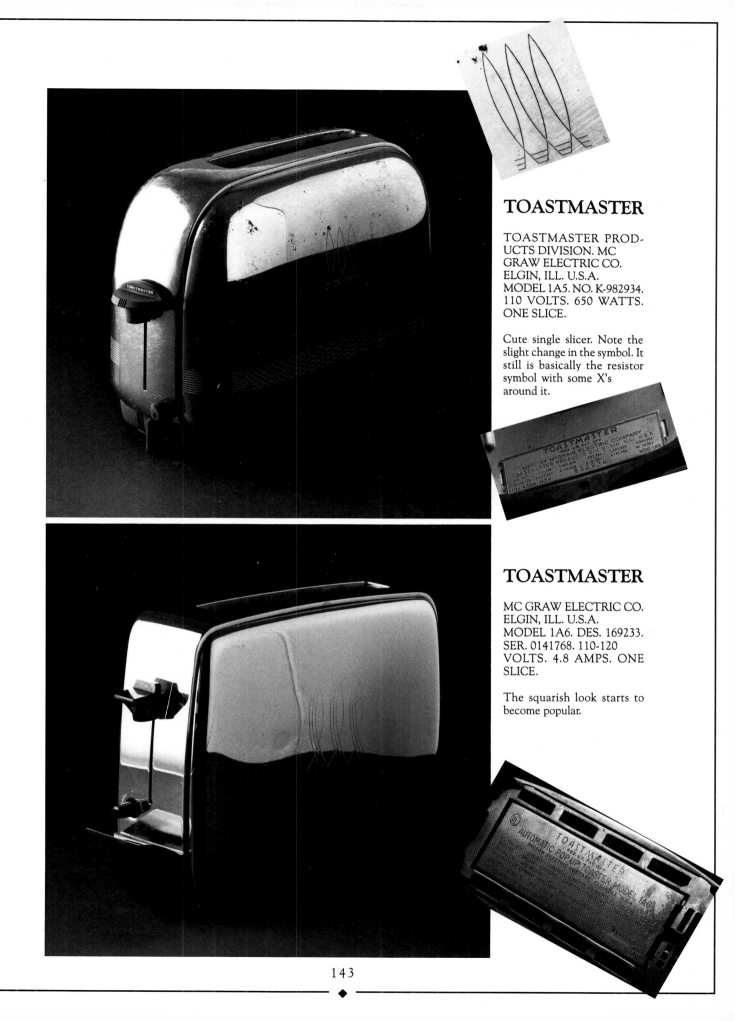

TOASTMASTER

TOASTMASTER PROD-
UCTS DIVISION. MC
GRAW ELECTRIC CO.
ELGIN, ILL. U.S.A.
MODEL 1A5. NO. K-982934.
110 VOLTS. 650 WATTS.
ONE SLICE.

Cute single slicer. Note the
slight change in the symbol. It
still is basically the resistor
symbol with some X's
around it.

TOASTMASTER

MC GRAW ELECTRIC CO.
ELGIN, ILL. U.S.A.
MODEL 1A6. DES. 169233.
SER. 0141768. 110-120
VOLTS. 4.8 AMPS. ONE
SLICE.

The squarish look starts to
become popular.

TOASTMASTER
SUPER DELUXE

TOASTMASTER PROD-
UCTS DIVISION. MC
GRAW ELECTRIC CO.
ELGIN, ILL. U.S.A.
MODEL 1B16. NO. 0280332.
110-120 VOLTS. 9.4 AMPS.
AC ONLY. TWO SLICES.

Gold three dimensional wheat
and name medallion on front.

TOASTMASTER

WATERS GENTER & CO.
MINNEAPOLIS, MINN.

MODEL 1D1. NO. 38105. 110
VOLTS. 2750 WATTS. PAT-
ENTS AUG. 16, '21. OCT. 18,
'21. FOUR SLICES.

Heavy cast aluminum with
mica windows. Restaurant version. Looks primitive but works
great. Has a timer. Load the
bread, set the timer, push down
the lever, wait. That's it.

TOASTWELL

THE TOASTWELL CO. ST.
LOUIS, MO.
CAT. NO. NS ATT4. CESA.
APP. NO. 3359. SERIAL NO.
436924. 115 VOLTS. 2500
WATTS. FOUR
SLICES.

Heavy steel commercial
model. Crumb tray.

TOASTMASTER AUTOMATIC POP-UP TOASTER

TOASTMASTER PROD
UCTS DIVISION. MC-
GRAW ELECTRIC CO.
ELGIN, ILL. U.S.A.
MODEL 1D2. NO. D 184294.
110-120 VOLTS. 2450
WATTS. FOUR SLICES.

The best toaster ever made. Big
heavy, sensitive controls. A real
winner. Also came in a two
slicer.

TOASTMASTER POWERMATIC SUPER DELUXE

TOASTMASTER PROD-
UCTS DIVISION. MC -
GRAW ELECTRIC CO.
ELGIN, ILL. U.S.A.
MODEL 1C4. 110-120
VOLTS. 12 AMPS. THREE
SLICES.

Unusual three slice toaster.
Still a quality product.

PORCELIER

PORCELIER MFG. CO.
GREENSBURG, PA.
CAT. NO. 5002. 115 VOLTS.
800 WATTS. TWO SLICES.

A porcelain toaster with a basket weave pattern and flowers
on the sides. One of four pat-
terns that were offered. Rare
to find because of its potential
for breakage and not too many
were made. Has a timer and
pops up when done. There
was an entire breakfast set
available but the toaster is the
most rare. You probably won't
find one of these at a
flea market, more
likely from a dealer and
at great expense.

1928
CHROME AUTO TOASTMAKER

BERSTED MFG. CO. CHICAGO, ILL.
MODEL 78. 115 VOLTS. 1100 WATTS. TWO SLICES.

This one looks like a rolling tea table on casters but it really doesn't roll. Not much style except for the feet. Has a timer graduated into seconds.

40s UTILITY ELECTRIC

UTILITY ELECTRIC CO. ST. LOUIS, MO. CAT. NO. 791. 110 VOLTS. 660 WATTS. H.E.P.C. APP. NO.3359. TWO SLICES.

Another train engine. It even has the side window, or a simulation of one, of a locomotive. Inexpensive toaster. Has a timer.

SON-CHIEF

SON-CHIEF ELECTRON-
ICS INC. WINSTED,
CONN.
SERIES 622. 115 VOLTS. 750
WATTS. AC ONLY. TWO
SLICES.

Another cheap toaster from
Son-Chief. This one's not long
on design either.

CORNET

CONNECTICUT APPLI-
ANCE CO. WINSTED,
CONN.
SERIES 612. 115 VOLTS. 750
WATTS. TWO SLICES.

Sure looks like another Son-
Chief but not marked as such.
Cheap but not a bad embossed
stripe design on ends.

MONITOR

MONITOR EQUIPMENT CORP. MADE IN U.S.A. NO. C4B. 110-120 VOLTS. 8 AMPS. AC ONLY. TWO SLICES.

Interesting light/dark push down handle. The logo on the side of the toaster is of a little man wearing big boots who appears to be skating but he has no skates. What's he doing? Reminds me of the Hold Heet Man who also is wearing big boots.

SUNBEAM

CHICAGO FLEXIBLE SHAFT CO. CHICAGO, ILL. MODEL T-1-E. DESIGN PATENT 98247. 110-120 VOLTS. 875 WATTS. TWO SLICES.

Elegant styling in a very well made toaster. Has a timer and a jewel on one side that glows red when the toaster is on.

SUNBEAM

CHICAGO FLEXIBLE
SHAFT CO. CHICAGO,
ILL.
MODEL T-I-E. (The "E" is
marked over.) DES. PAT.
98247. 110-120 VOLTS. 875
WATTS. TWO SLICES.

Same toaster as previous page
with slight design changes.
More Deco influence in this
model. Must be using the same
base as the other design just
striking out part of the model
number. Has a jewel that
glows red when the heat is on.
Very well made with large
range of browning adjust-
ments.

SUNBEAM

SUNBEAM CORP. CHI
CAGO, U.S.A. TORONTO,
CANADA.
MODEL T-9. CSA AP
PROVAL. 8402. 110-120
VOLTS. 1100 WATTS.
TWO SLICES.

A great looking Deco toaster.
Nice jewel in the side which
glows red when the heat is on.
Classic lines with a well done
Deco design on the opposite
side of the jewel. A variation
of this design will be used on
later toasters as well. They
must have made a billion of
these, you see them every
where. Wildly overpriced at
most Flea Markets. But they
look good on the counter so
they are very popular.

PROCTOR TOASTER
WITH COLOR
GUARD

PROCTOR ELECTRIC CO. PHILADELPHIA, PA. U.S.A.
MODEL 1467A. 110-120 VOLTS. 1000 WATTS. AC ONLY.
TWO SLICES.

Color Guard is Proctor's browning heat sensor that acts as a non
ticking timer. Wheat design on the sides. OK toaster. Big wattage in a two slicer for home use.

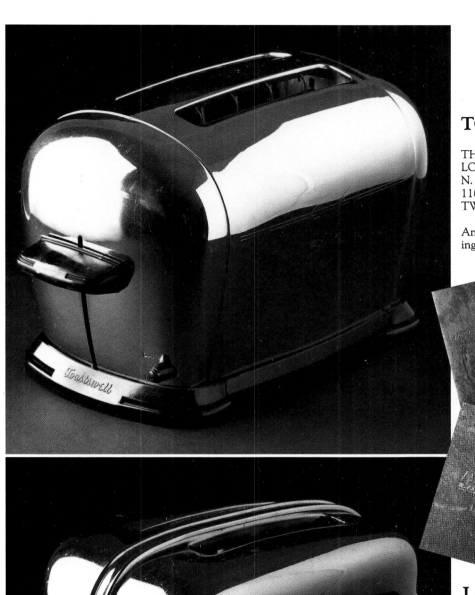

TOASTWELL

THE TOASTWELL CO. ST.
LOUIS, MO.
N. 222-48. APP. NO. 3359.
110 VOLTS. 825 WATTS.
TWO SLICES.

Another Choo-Choo. Nothing special.

LASKO
AUTOMATIC
POP-UP
TOASTER

LASKO METAL PROD
UCTS INC. WEST
CHESTER, PA.
MODEL NO. 8. 115 VOLTS.
1000 WATTS. AC OF DC.
PAT. PENDING. 730385.
TWO SLICES.

Has the sleek look of a bulbous
Pullman Sleeper Car or the
bumper of a fat Buick. A great
look! Unfortunately my example of this toaster is rather
rusty.

TOASTWELL

THE TOASTWELL CO.
ST. LOUIS, MO.
NO. 350. 110-120 VOLTS.
920 WATTS. TWO
SLICES.

A fat chrome football. The
light/dark control is in the
push down knob.

GENERAL ELECTRIC

GENERAL ELECTRIC CO.
BRIDGEPORT, CONN.
CAT. NO. 159T77. DES.
133315. 115 VOLTS. 1150
WATTS. TWO SLICES.

An almost patriotic motif on
the sides. If there were an
eagle holding the olive
branch and the arrow it
would be complete. I guess
it's really sheaves of wheat
though. Has a keep warm
option and lots of buttons
to play with.

MAGIC MAID

MAGIC MAID DIVISION.
SON-CHIEF ELECTRICS
INC. WINSTED, CONN.
U.S.A.
SERIES 666. 115 VOLTS.
750 WATTS. TWO
SLICES.

A cartoon locomotive. I just
wanna squeeze that nose!
The side design is another
electrical symbol. Better
work than most of the Son-
Chief products.

1950s
MANNING
BOWMAN

MANNING BOWMAN &
CO. MERIDAN, CONN.
U.S.A.
#2-50. MODEL 116. 110-
120 VOLTS. 10 AMPS.
TWO SLICES.

Timer. Wild design on sides.
Another clown toaster.

PROCTOR

PROCTOR ELEC-
TRIC CO. PHILA
DELPHIA 40, PENN.
MODEL 1481. 110-120
VOLTS. 1000
WATTS. TWO
SLICES.

Slick, sleek Pullman
Car that can glide
through the scenery
without rustling a leaf
or ruffling a feather. A
real smooth toaster.
Some models had cop-
per bottoms others had
black bottoms.

KENMORE

KENMORE "OUR
OWN TRADE
MARK" (NO MEN-
TION OF SEARS &
ROEBUCK)
MODEL 344-6332. SE-
RIAL NO. 53. 110-120
VOLTS. 1200
WATTS. 10.4 AMPS.
TWO SLICES.

Came in a variety of
colors. Small knob miss-
ing from this example.
Medium grade toaster.
Great color.

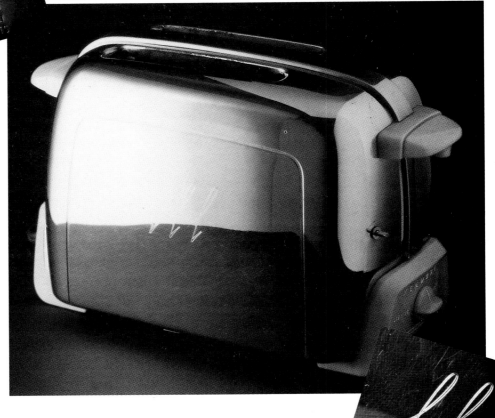

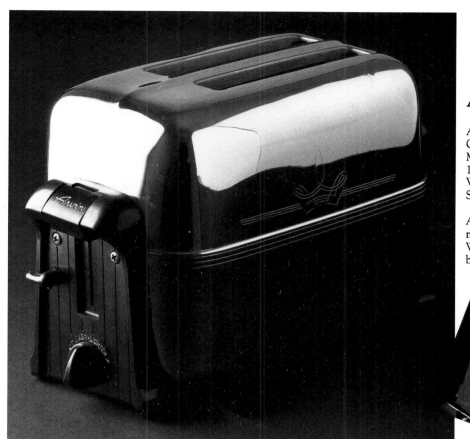

ARVIN

ARVIN INDUSTRIES INC.
COLUMBUS, IND. U.S.A.
MODEL 4200. SERIAL NO.
123. 110-120 VOLTS. 1170
WATTS. 10.2 AMPS. TWO
SLICES.

A company that's known
more for radios than toasters.
Well made. Nicely molded
bakelite trim and knobs.

WESTINGHOUSE

WESTINGHOUSE.
MANSFIELD, OHIO. U.S.A.
CAT. NO. TO-71. DES. 150-
134. #J203223. TWO
SLICES.

Big fat yet slick toaster. Nice
design stamping on the side,
much like heraldry or a coat
of arms in old England.

GENERAL MILLS

GENERAL MILLS INC.
MINNEAPOLIS, MINN.
U.S.A.
CAT. NO. GM5A. NO.
CD (?) 110-120 VOLTS.
1200 WATTS. TWO
SLICES.

An upside down Sunbeam
T-9. Big molded bakelite
ends and base as one
piece. Not bad for Betty
Crocker.

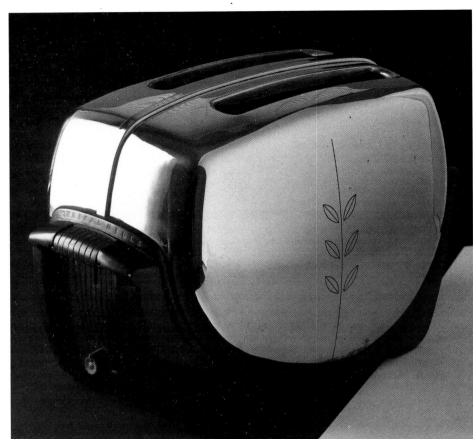

WESTINGHOUSE

WESTINGHOUSE.
MANSFIELD, OHIO.
CAT. NO. TD414. 115
VOLTS. 1110 WATTS.
TWO SLICES.

Cleans lines but not very
interesting although it
does have one end that's
rounded. Another high
wattage toaster.

WEST BEND

THE WEST BEND
COMPANY. WEST
BEND, WISCONSIN.
U.S.A.
MODEL 3232E. SERIES
36K. 110-120 VOLTS.
1050 WATTS. AC
ONLY. TWO SLICES.

Gold three dimensional
wheat design on the sides.

WESTINGHOUSE

THE WEST BEND COM-
PANY. WEST BEND, WIS-
CONSIN. U.S.A.
CAT. NO. TO-5422-P. 115
VOLTS. 1320 WATTS. TWO
SLICES.

A pink George Jetson locomotive toaster.

MISCELLANEOUS

Grab Bag

11

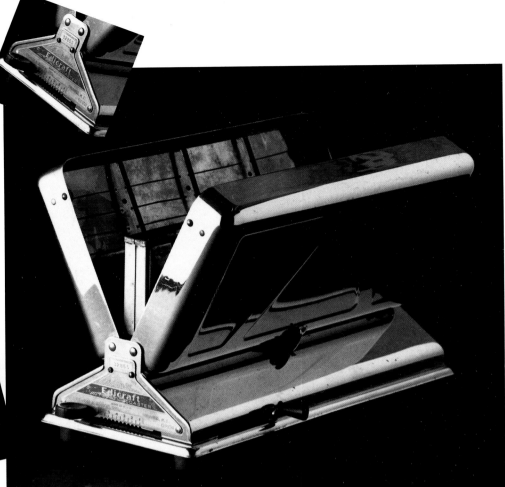

THOMAS A. EDISON EDICRAFT

THOMAS A. EDISON INC. ORANGE, N. J. SERIAL NO. 32855. TWO SLICES.

Complicated mechanism. Very well made. Has a timer that opens the jaw like toaster when the toast is done. Closing lever on the side claps the toaster closed.

Courtesy of Joe Lukach

MANNING BOWMAN

MANNING BOWMAN & CO. MERIDIAN, CONN. USA
SERIAL NO. 11-25. PATENT 1-27-25.ONE SLICE.

Well made. Push the end button and the toast is pushed up. Can be used with doors for moist toast of without doors for crisp toast. It would be difficult to change the doors once you had made your initial decision without letting the toaster cool down.

Courtesy of Joe Lukach

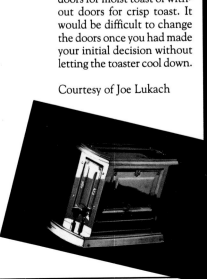

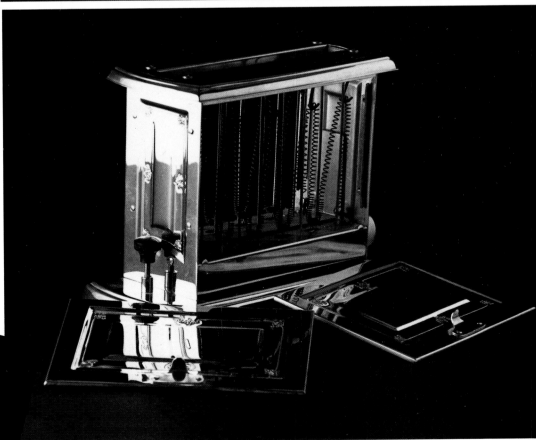

COMMANDER TOASTER

WHARTON MFG. CO.
PHILADELPHIA, PA.
TWO SLICES

A brute of a toaster, the name is well founded. Heavy duty! Knob on front rotates and opens the heavy doors to reveal the toast in its basket holders. A gigantic push button on and off switch occupies the front, later models did away with this large switch. Has three elements. One of the heaviest toasters known. Nickel plated, with knobs and handles available in Catalin (?) in Russian onyx, jade, crimson, and black colors.
$12.50 in 1929.

Courtesy of Joe Lukach

DOMINION

DOMINION MFG. INC. MANSFIELD, OHIO
STYLE #1105. 110-120 VOLTS. 660 WATTS. TWO SLICES.

Not a Pop-Up. The knob on the end is used to pull the toast up. Cheap.

UTILITY

UTILITY ELECTRIC CO. ST. LOUIS, MO.
110 VOLTS. 900 WATTS. TWO SLICES.

Not a Pop-Up. Each side is controlled by a sliding knob which you push the toast up with. Nice stamping. Looks like boiler plate with its rivets on the ends.

UTILITY

UTILITY ELECTRIC CO. ST. LOUIS, MO.
CAT. NO. 780. 110 VOLTS. 660 WATTS. TWO SLICES.

Not a Pop-Up. Timer rings a bell when done and shuts off the toaster, you must pull the handle up to get at the toast. Elegant embossed sides.

HOTPOINT

GENERAL ELECTRIC.
GENERAL ELECTRIC CO.
BRIDGEPORT, CONN.
ONTARIO, CALIF. U.S.A.
CAT. NO. 129T41. 115
VOLTS. 850 WATTS. TWO
SLICES.

This one looks like a flopper but isn't. To operate it you turn the end knob, this opens both sides of the toaster at once. Inside are three elements, one in each door and a center one. The toast is separated from its element by the basket which positions it for easy grabbing. Heavy toaster. Has a bi-metal thermostat.

HOTPOINT? UNKNOWN, NO BASE ON TOASTER

Probably a Hotpoint, has all the same mechanics as the previous toaster.

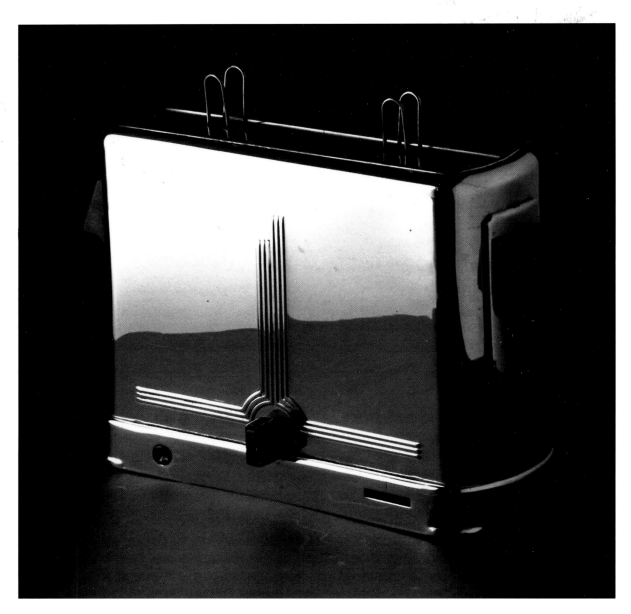

TEL-A-MATIC. K&M

KNAPP MONARCH CO. ST. LOUIS, MO.
CAT. NO. 537. 115 VOLTS. 800 WATTS. TWO SLICES.

Not a Pop-Up. A Long Slot toaster. Turn the knob on the
front and the toast is lifted up in its basket.

NOVELTIES

Kids Stuff

12

EXCEL

EXCEL ELECTRIC CO. MUNCIE, IND. U.S.A.

Kids toaster that's real and works but toasts bread lousy. I
guess safety wasn't paramount when this toaster was made.

LADY JUNIOR MINIATURE
ELECTRIC TOASTER

A METROPOLITAN PRODUCT. "EDUCATIONAL
ELECTRIC PLAYTHINGS"
CAT. NO. 350. 110 VOLTS. 180 WATTS.

This toaster works but doesn't brown the bread evenly.

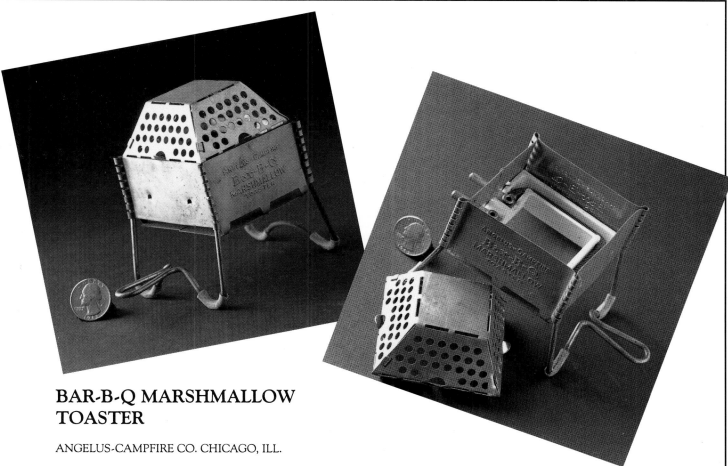

BAR-B-Q MARSHMALLOW TOASTER

ANGELUS-CAMPFIRE CO. CHICAGO, ILL.

This little toaster doesn't toast bread. It toasts marshmallows but I couldn't resist showing it. It's also not a kid's toaster if you believe the photographs on the box. There are adults dressed in cocktail party attire toasting marshmallows around this toaster, but it looks much bigger in the ad than in real life. Two metal forks originally came with the toaster.

CONTROLA

Controla is stamped in the side of this kids toaster. Chrome sides and fake wood grain ends. It doesn't toast the bread it kinda warms it.

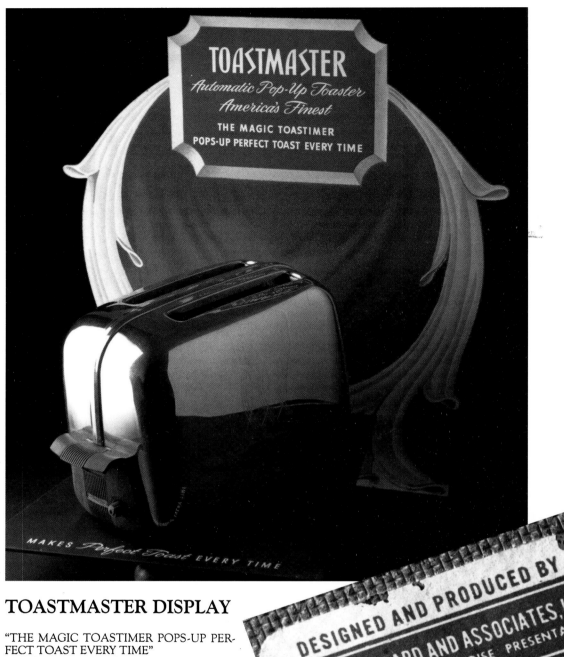

TOASTMASTER DISPLAY

"THE MAGIC TOASTIMER POPS-UP PER-
FECT TOAST EVERY TIME"
DESIGNED AND PRODUCED BY
W.L.STENSGAARD AND ASSOCIATES, INC.
CHICAGO. NEW YORK. OAKLAND.

I have never had the occasion to use the word
"TOASTIMER" before. Finally I'm satisfied. The
toaster shown may not be the one intended for
this display.

Courtesy of Doug Huse

CANVAS TOASTER

MFG. BY E. TOWNSEND ARTMAN, CHICAGO, ILL. U.S.A.

Toaster and bread made of #10 cotton canvas. Non electric. Has fake timer, bell, cord, and toast.

CRUMBS

Archeologists tell us that bread was toasted in Ancient Egypt 4600 years ago. Loaves of bread were found in the tombs of the dead Pharaohs and were almost identical to the bread made in Egypt today. So maybe toasted bread in Egypt today tastes like toasted bread in Egypt 4600 years ago.

Some say the ancient Romans discovered that burned crusts improved the quality of the wine. The wine often needed help.

The expression to "Make a Toast" or to "Toast" someone comes to us from history also. The English are credited with inventing the phrase. During the time of the French revolution the toast is mentioned in Alexandre Dumas' *Dictionary of Cuisine* published by Simon and Schuster, Inc., New York. The tradition was to put toast in the bottom of a beer pot and pour beer over it. Each person took a drink and pronounced a "Toast" passing the cup to the next. The last person toasting got to eat the toast.

Sometime in the early 1800s the wrought iron holder (a long wrought iron fork with a basket at the end) was in common use over the open kitchen fire. Each one was hand made and are quite collectible today.

Around the time of the American Civil War things heated up and not just on the battlefield. Wire and tinware toaster stands appeared in droves and were sold in general stores and hawked by the "Tin Man" on every frontier post in America. They were just wire stands balancing the bread over a wood stove until it toasted. They supported four slices and looked much like a small Pilgrim hat or a chimney with wire supports. They toasted America's bread consistently until the early 1900s. With the advent of electricity things changed, but these stands were still on the market in the 70s-80s. Who preferred them over the many electric toasters available, is anybody's guess. Maybe folks without electricity, you say. In any case, they are still found for sale at every flea market in the United States today.

White Wonder Bread™ was used for toasting tests in Chicago. In New Orleans white Bunny Bread™ was used. Both have a soft feel and fine texture.

There are still lots of toasters out there to be collected. By the time this book is printed I will have found at least one more to add to its chapters, but I can't hold up production forever to get that last one in, because, after all, there never is a last one.